BUSINESS WRITING FOR HOSPITALITY

Vivienne J. Wildes, Ph.D.
The Pennsylvania State University

Peter D. Nyheim
The Pennsylvania State University

PEARSON

Prentice
Hall

UPPER SADDLE RIVER, NEW JERSEY
COLUMBUS, OHIO

Library of Congress Cataloging-in-Publication Data
Wildes, Vivienne J.
  Business writing for hospitality / Vivienne J. Wildes, Peter Nyheim.
    p. cm.
  Includes index.
  ISBN-13: 978-0-13-171571-4
  ISBN-10: 0-13-171571-2
  1. Hospitality industry—Study and teaching.   2. Business writing.   I. Nyheim, Peter.   II. Title.
  TX911.5.W55 2008
  338.4′791—dc22

                                                                    2008007798

Editor In Chief: Vernon Anthony
Acquisitions Editor: William Lawrensen
Editorial Assistant: Lara Dimmick
Media Project Manager: Karen Bretz
Director of Marketing: David Gessell
Senior Marketing Manager: Leigh Ann Sims
Marketing Assistant: Les Roberts
Production Manager: Kathy Sleys
Creative Director: Jayne Conte
Cover Design: Jayne Kelly
Cover Illustration/Photo: Scott Pitts © Dorling Kindersley
Full-Service Project Management/Composition: Saraswathi Muralidhar/GGS Book Services PMG
Printer/Binder: Courier/Stoughton

Pearson Education Ltd., London
Pearson Education Singapore, Pte. Ltd
Pearson Education Canada, Inc.
Pearson Education–Japan
Pearson Education Australia PTY, Limited

Pearson Education North Asia, Ltd., Hong Kong
Pearson Educación de Mexico, S.A. de C.V.
Pearson Education Malaysia, Pte. Ltd.
Pearson Education Upper Saddle River, New Jersey

10 9 8 7 6 5 4 3 2 1
ISBN-13: 978-0-13-171571-4
ISBN-10: 0-13-171571-2

For the Crones,
in order of appearance:
Dona, Val, and Beth

—Vivienne Wildes

For April

—Peter Nyheim

Contents

Preface

E-mails, memos, purchase orders, requests for proposals, employee evaluations, and guest correspondences are just a few examples of the written documents used in the hospitality industry. What is often overlooked is that these documents represent you and your company. Writers beware! The impression made by the written word is often permanent or expensive to fix.

In any profession, writing is one of the oldest and most important means of communicating. In the fast-moving hospitality industry, "good" writing is sometimes sacrificed in the name of speed. This should not be the case. This text endeavors to aid current and future managers by giving them some of the tools and skills necessary to successful writing.

This text covers writing in the hospitality industry in general. It is organized around the documents found within the various departments of a hotel or restaurant, using samples from these departments that provide both pertinent and useful information. The text can be used both for teaching and as a reference tool. Although the chapters can be read in any order, we recommend starting with Chapter 1 (grammar review) before going on to any of the others.

Chapter 1, the review of grammar, is important because correct grammar lays the foundation for good writing. The chapter covers active and passive voice, pronoun agreement, punctuation, and much more. It emphasizes important grammatical points (and errors!) to provide the requisite knowledge and a basic foundation.

Chapters 2 through 7 cover the various aspects of writing in the hospitality industry. Each of the chapters begins with a story that illustrates how and why the types of writing covered in that chapter are required. For example, Chapter 2 covers administrative documents—formality, overused words, correct salutations, etc.

The department of human resources requires some special types of writing, which are covered in Chapter 3. This department is paper-intensive and, therefore, writing-intensive. Chapter 3 covers writing that applies to job postings and job descriptions, letters of recommendation, and so forth.

Chapter 4 concerns the sales and catering departments. A business could have the best food and beverage service around, but an error in correspondence to a potential client can lose an account.

Chapter 5 details the writing used in the rooms division of a hotel. Proper composition of the "daily log," revenue recording, and guest messages are discussed in this chapter.

Chapter 6 covers the on-site food and beverage department. Documents discussed include: checklists, invitations, purchase orders, and displays for guests.

The topic of Chapter 7 is purchasing, specifically from the standpoint of purchasing technology. How to present requirements to vendors is depicted here in the form of a sample request for proposal (RFP) for point-of-sale technology.

Finally, the appendix to the book contains a detailed training program for wait staff that is intended to illustrate the importance of organization and checklists. These are, of course, important aspects of good writing, but the training program is an added bonus feature of this book. We hope you can make good use of the attention to detail.

We hope you find this text useful, and we wish you good luck in your careers!

We appreciate the contributions of the reviewers of this project: Donna Campbell, Washington State University; Dougal Gray, Columbus State Community College; Bradford Hudson, Boston University; Dena Woerner, Indiana University Purdue University Fort Wayne.

Acknowledgments

The authors would like to acknowledge those who supported their efforts in producing *Business Writing for Hospitality*.

A special thanks to Joe Beddall, Alex, and Abbie. Thank you to Joyce Nicholas for her persistence to getting the idea to the page.

We would like to thank Sodexho for allowing the reprints of their internship brochures.

We are grateful to the director, faculty, staff, and students in the School of Hospitality Management at Penn State University for their support and good hallway humor.

Thank you to our extended families for their encouragement over the years and for future projects.

Thank you to the many recruiters of hospitality students for reviewing early editions of the manuscript and for their continued insistence on the need for good writing.

This book is much improved because of the editors and staff at Prentice Hall and GGS Book Services PMG. Thank you to Kathy Sleys, Project Manager. A special thanks to Cindy Miller at GGS for her patience and understanding whilst time got in the way. Thank you to Dan Trudden for his editorial assistance, especially of the grammar chapter. Thanks to Les Roberts for his marketing and publicity efforts. And finally, thank you to the India team, particularly Saraswathi Muralidhar for keeping the press rolling. The book is all the better for your efforts.

—Vivienne Wildes

Peter Nyheim

1 ‖ GRAMMAR

The hospitality industry, like most, requires some ability to communicate. Correct grammar is crucial to getting the message across. Simply put, correct grammar and spelling make the difference between a clear, coherent, and well-expressed idea and a message that comes across as tongue-tied, mumbled, confused, and rambling. Grammar pulls the message together. Grammar is the basis of good writing, education, research, and expression.

Introduction

Correct grammar is essential to anyone who wishes to appear professional. This chapter considers style, appearance, punctuation, and tone. Certain rules apply to business writing; many were constructed years ago and are still in use today. Most rules are a matter of common sense and unless you are writing cutting-edge fiction, it is best to learn and follow them. When in doubt about something, look it up. Numerous reference guides to professional writing, dictionaries, thesauri, and secretarial handbooks are available, and any good office has at least a few of these at hand.

RULES

Rules are statements about how a language works. Some rules are very clear; other rules are more problematic. Reading about rules or explanations can help, but the most useful way to learn is to pay attention to the English you hear and read. Concentrating and focusing on others' speaking and writing helps you get a "feel" for both good and bad grammar.

Numerous web sites and books help sort through rules, explain commonly confused words, provide useful grammar tips, and give sound spelling advice. You can learn plenty about rules from reference books, particularly dictionaries. Interestingly, those who most appreciate words (known as *wordsmiths*) have the largest accumulation of reference books on their bookshelves; however, even if you write just a little bit, a few good reference books—and especially one good dictionary—should grace your desk.

The good news about grammar is that it can be learned. It is also true that those grammar rules we should have learned in eighth grade come back to haunt our attempts at written and spoken communication. Rather than bemoaning what you could have known if you had paid attention or had had a good eighth-grade teacher, you can still easily learn and use proper grammar in the workplace.

One word—*feed*—has the following definitions in an online dictionary:

feed /fiːd/ *verb, noun*

■ verb (fed, fed /fed/)

GIVE / EAT FOOD

1. feed sb/sth (on) sth | feed sth to sb/sth to give food to a person or an animal:
   [vn] *Have you fed the cat yet?* • *The baby can't feed itself yet* (= can't put food into its own mouth). • *The cattle are fed on barley.* • [vnn, vn] *The cattle are fed barley.* • *The barley is fed to the cattle.*

2. • [v] (of a baby or an animal) to eat food:
   Slugs and snails feed at night.
   —see also feed on / off sth

3. [vn] to provide food for a family or group of people:
   They have a large family to feed. • *There's enough here to feed an army.*

PLANT

4. [vn] to give a plant a special substance to make it grow:
   Feed the plants once a week.

GIVE ADVICE / INFORMATION

5. feed sb sth | feed sth to sb to give advice, information, etc. to sb/sth:
   [vnn, vn] *We are constantly fed gossip and speculation by the media.* • *Gossip and speculation are constantly fed to us by the media.*

SUPPLY

6. [vn] feed A (with B) | feed B into A to supply sth to sb/sth:
   The electricity line is fed with power through an underground cable. • *Power is fed into the electricity line through an underground cable.* • *The lake is fed by a river.*

PUT INTO MACHINE

7. [vn] feed A (with B) | feed B into A | feed sth (into / through sth) to put or push sth into or through a machine:
   He fed coins into the meter. • *He fed the meter with coins.* • *The information was fed into the data store.* • *The fabric is fed through the machine.*

SATISFY NEED

8. [vn] to satisfy a need, desire, etc. and keep it strong:
   For drug addicts, the need to feed the addiction takes priority over everything else.

• ˌfeed your ˈface
  (informal, usually disapproving) to eat a lot of food or too much food—more at bite *verb*.

• ˌfeed ˈback (into / to sth)
  to have an influence on the development of sth by reacting to it in some way:
  What the audience tells me feeds back into my work.

• ˌfeed (sth) ↔ ˈback (to sb)
  to give information or opinions about sth, especially so that it can be improved:
  Test results will be fed back to the schools.

• ˈfeed into sth
  to have an influence on the development of sth:
  The report's findings will feed into company policy.

• ˈfeed on / off sth
  1 (of an animal) to eat sth:
  Butterflies feed on the flowers of garden plants.

  2 (often disapproving) to become stronger because of sth else: *Racism feeds on fear.* • *He feeds off the work and reputation of others.*

• ˌfeed ˈthrough (to sb/sth)
  to reach sb/sth after going through a process or system:

It will take time for the higher rates to feed through to investors.

- **,feed sb ↔ 'up**
(BrE) to give a lot of food to sb to make them fatter or stronger

■ noun

MEAL FOR BABY / ANIMAL

1. [C] a meal of milk for a young baby; a meal for an animal:
her morning feed

FOR ANIMALS / PLANTS

2. [U, C] food for animals or plants:
winter feed for the horses • liquid tomato feed • a sack of feed

FOR MACHINE

3. [U] material supplied to a machine

4. [C] a pipe, device, etc. which supplies a machine with sth:
the cold feed to the water cylinder • The printer has an automatic paper feed.

LARGE MEAL

5. [C] (informal) a large meal:
They needed a bath and a good feed.

TELEVISION PROGRAMMES

6. [U] (NAmE) television programmes that are sent from a central station to other stations in a network; the system of sending out these programmes:
network feed

© Oxford University Press, 2005.

STYLE

Two big questions guide **style** choices: "What is it you want to say?" and "Who is your audience?"

Style can change from one message to another; nonetheless, style is critical to the message. The reader's perception of a written message is crucial to the effect of the message itself. If someone does not "get it," then you have failed in your delivery. In other words, own your message.

So, the first thing you need to ask yourself is, "What is the purpose of this piece of information that I'm about to send forward?" You don't want to appear apologetic, for instance, when your real need is to explain a procedure. Likewise, when answering a letter of complaint, you don't want to come off as dogmatic.

DIFFERENT STYLES FOR DIFFERENT PURPOSES

Requesting information
Providing information
Complaining diplomatically

Praising
Explaining procedure

What Is It You Want to Say?

Two considerations in defining what you want to say are the subject and the point.

The Subject

The subject is the general topic that you're writing about. Perhaps you are requesting a special delivery, or your supervisor has asked you to draft a letter of praise to an employee. You might be writing a press release to announce a new menu. The main idea is to decide what exactly you are writing about.

The Point

The reasoning behind a particular piece of writing is the point. You might ask yourself, "What is it I want the reader to come away with?" For example, if you are writing an announcement about a new menu, you might explain why the chef decided to put it together. Is it lighter fare? A seasonal menu? A tie-in with another partner? Expansion? The subject of this example is the new menu. The point is to make employees aware that the menu will change and that training programs will be offered.

The point will help to organize the rest of your document. Write it down in one sentence to clarify what exactly you want the reader to take away from your message.

Who Is Your Audience?

The reader is really the most important person to consider when you are writing a document, letter, memo, or anything else. In business writing, you are not writing for yourself; rather, you are writing for an end user. This can be a client, guest, employee, colleague, or distributor.

Decide to whom you are writing. If you are writing for more than one audience, you can use a broader approach. You may also decide to tweak the document to create several different versions that can be sent to different audiences.

Questions for picturing your audience:

What do they need to come away with?	Are you addressing one person or a group?
What is in it for them?	
What is their level of education/ knowledge?	What is the follow-up?

TONE

Think of a time when you came away from reading a letter or memo with the feeling of "Eeeewww!" You may have decided right then and there to toss the paper aside or to delete the message. Perhaps you decided that no way would you participate in that activity. Now remember a letter or memo from which you came away with the feeling of "Yes!—That is worthwhile information!" Perhaps you immediately signed up, sent the memo along to a friend or colleague, or made a copy and decided to keep the information.

Which type of reaction do you want your information to receive?

So many times, how a person reacts to a piece of writing depends on the **tone**. The idea behind tone is to "take the high road." Be professional. Be polite. There's a rule of thumb that says if you think 20 percent of the people who read your document will feel confused, insulted, or put off, then rewrite it. One of the best ways to avoid mistakes in tone is to have at least two or three colleagues or friends read the document before you send it. If you have time, you might want to put the piece aside for a day or two, and then re-read it with special attention to tone. This is especially helpful when writing something that could prove hurtful or have potentially negative consequences.

Evaluate the "feeling" of the word choices. Make sure that they really say what you want to say accurately and precisely. And, of course, use good manners.

WORDS THAT EQUATE TO "TONE"

quality	attitude	air
manner	nature	climate
character	feeling	mood

CLARITY

Clarity in writing refers to saying exactly what you intend to say so that others will understand you. Avoid jargon and insider language. When using acronyms, be sure they are defined earlier in the document. Clarity is a cornerstone of good business writing. Articulate your information precisely.

VOICE

Voice is the way you sound on paper. Weird as it may feel, the best way to hear your written voice is to read what you write aloud. Yes, read your paper to yourself, a colleague, or a friend. Only then do you get to hear whether what you intended to say is accurate.

Active vs. Passive Voice

There are two types of voice in the English language: **passive voice** and **active voice**.

In sentences written in the active voice, the subject acts. That is, the subject performs the action (expressed in the verb). For example, an active-voice sentence might read: The boy threw the ball. *The boy* (subject) *threw* (verb) *the ball.*

In sentences written in the passive voice, the subject is acted upon. That is, the subject receives the action expressed in the verb. For example, a passive-voice sentence might read: *The ball* (subject) *was thrown* (verb) *by the boy.*

In general, try to use active rather than passive voice in your wiring. Active voice adds clarity and forcefulness to a sentence. It eliminates needless words.

Example:

> *Passive:* The piano is played by Mary.
> *Active:*   Mary plays the piano.

Many people simply do not understand active and passive voice. The idea is really quite simple; the following chart explains the differences between them:

> *Active Voice (the subject performs the action)*
>
> The boy threw the ball.
> The chef created the menu.
> We made a mistake.
> XYZ Corporation bought 500 acres of cilantro fields.
>
> *Passive Voice (the subject receives the action)*
>
> The ball was thrown by the boy.
> The menu was created by the chef.
> A mistake was made by the corporation.
> Five hundred acres of cilantro fields were bought by XYZ Corporation.

THE OPENING PARAGRAPH

The opening paragraph sets the tone for your writing. The initial sentence should be clear and outline the basics: who, what, where, when, how. Make the first sentence interesting, if possible. Get to the point quickly and make the flow easy to follow.

The opening paragraph should grab your readers' attention and guide them through the points. When reviewing your document, don't be afraid to fine-tune and clarify the points made. Sometimes it is a good idea to cover the main points within the first one or two paragraphs and then return to each point later in the document with fuller explanation.

CREATIVE OPENERS

Quote	Story
Question	Image
Personal experience	

APPEARANCE

An adage from the business world holds true for written correspondence. That is, there is only one chance to make a first impression. The appearance of your document should reflect the standards of your company. Appearance includes the visual format of your document, the layout and design of logos, the quality of paper, the appearance of envelopes or enclosures, and the quality of handouts.

Appearance is enhanced by simplicity. For example, one-sentence paragraphs can be very effective in writing memos. Boldface, italics, and underlining provide visual impact that can catch the eye of readers or stress a particular point. Bullet points, lists, boxes, and charts are graphic devices that express information visually. Computers make these tools easy to use.

Subheadings are effective ways to segment information. For example, a memo explaining how to use a certain machine can break up the information into a point-by-point process using subheadings.

PUNCTUATION

No discussion of grammar is complete without a discussion of punctuation. Basic punctuation marks include the period, the exclamation point, the comma, the question mark, and quotation marks. These marks are road signs. They guide the reader through the sentence and clarify exactly what you are trying to say. Punctuation points readers in the direction you need them to go.

Other punctuation marks that are sometimes used can make for more interesting reading. These include the dash, semicolon, colon, and ellipsis.

The Period

- The most basic of punctuation tools, the period, is used at the end of a complete thought. Use a period at the end of a complete sentence that is a statement. This type of statement is known as a *declarative sentence*.

  Example: The food is good.
  Example: The butler was there when the patron fell from his chair.
  Example: I like amusement parks.

- If the last word in the sentence is an abbreviation that ends in a period, do not follow it with another period.

  Example: She is a Ph.D. She is also my sister.
  Example: Please buy these paper products from the store: paper towels, construction paper, tissues, etc. I will handle the vegetable list.

Exclamation Point

- An exclamation point is used at the end of a direct command or statement. It is more forceful than a period and adds emphasis. The exclamation point can be used at the end of an *exclamatory sentence* to add excitement.
- Exclamation points are also used with direct commands to express urgency. The use of an exclamation point to express urgency makes the sentence an *imperative sentence*.

  Example: The food is good! (exclamatory)
  Example: The butler was there! (exclamatory)
  Example: Sit down! (imperative)
  Example: She yelled, "Fire!" (imperative)

Declarative sentences state an idea.
Example: New Orleans is a jazz town.

Exclamatory sentences add emphasis.
Example: A good time was had by all!

Imperative   sentences   give   direct information.
Example: Consider the guests!

The Comma
The Comma, a powerful grammar tool, is used for many purposes.

- Commas are used to separate items in a list. Commas are optional before or after the last word—the idea is to be consistent with your choice throughout your writing.

  Example:

  We will eat turkey, stuffing, and mashed potatoes.
  We will eat turkey, stuffing and mashed potatoes.

- Commas are used to join two or more independent clauses into a compound sentence. They must be used before conjunctions such as like, and, but, yet, for, so.

  Example: Alex was startled by the noise, and she ran outside to see what was the matter.

- Commas are used to set off *nonrestrictive clauses* that begin with which, who, whom, and whose.

  Examples:

  My sister, <u>who</u> lives in Idaho, came for a visit. (your only sister—nonrestrictive clause)
  My sister who lives in Idaho came for a visit. (one of two sisters in two different states—restrictive clause)
  The report, <u>which</u> was well documented, was discussed with considerable emotions. (the only report—nonrestrictive clause)

  Be careful:

  The report <u>that</u> the committee submitted was well documented. (<u>That</u> is restrictive and does not require a comma.)

- Commas are used to set off long, dependent introductory elements.

  Examples:

  Frightened by the movie, Abbie couldn't sleep.
  Although he would have preferred not to, Paul drove us home.

- Commas are used to set off parenthetical statements, interjections, and transitional elements.

  Examples:

  O.J. Simpson, many believed, was guilty of his wife's murder.
  Well, I have got to get going.
  We shall, however, return to this issue at a later date.

- Commas are used to set off appositives—nouns or phrases that add information about the preceding noun.

  Examples:

  My husband, David, wrote a letter to our congressman.

His second novel, a detective story with psychological overtones, was influenced by the work of Dostoyevsky.

Be careful:
My son Michael was the first to arrive. (one of two or more)
O'Neill's play *Anna Christie* was revived on Broadway.

- Commas are used to set off quotations.

  Example: Ellen shouted, "You'll never get away with this!"

The Question Mark

- The question mark is used when you are seeking information. An *interrogative sentence* asks a direct question and always ends in a question mark.

  Examples:

  Where were you on the night of October 5th, 2008? (interrogative sentence)
  How many people are planning summer vacations?
  Did the quality inspection team make it to your establishment on time?

- Question marks can also be used at the end of a declarative sentence.

  Examples:

  It seems many people are planning vacations in July, correct?
  The deliveries are arriving before the staff is scheduled to accept them, is that true?

Quotation Marks

Quotation marks are used to set off a quoted speech, a phrase, or a word. They are used in pairs and are also called quotes, speech marks, or inverted commas. There are a number of rules that govern the use of quotation marks with other punctuation.

- Periods and commas that punctuate the surrounding sentence go inside quotation marks.

  Examples:

  The oven degree will change from "350 degrees" to "375 degrees," and the "beep" will sound.
  The director said "Congratulations."

- If a question mark belongs to a quotation, the question mark is placed inside the quotation marks. *Note*: British usage may be different.

  Example: Mark asked, "Will you be there to close the shop?"

- When a question is embedded within a question, one question mark is placed inside the quotation mark.

  Example: Did you say, "How can I make things better?"

- Some quotes occur within quotes, in which case single quotation marks are used for the embedded quote.

  Example: The corporate officer said, "Sally specifically said 'I will be there until the end,' on Tuesday."

- Quotations are used to set off a direct quotation.

  Example: "What is the point of this conversation?" she asked.

Dashes

Dashes are a fun and unique way to set off explanatory details. It is best to use dashes sparingly—that is, don't overuse them—since they are "special" and used for impact.

- Dashes help to separate an opening list from a complete statement.

  Example: Tom, Ralph, and Glenn—these were my true friends.

- Dashes set off explanatory details, such as an explanation that comes between a subject and a verb.

  Example: The two brothers—supposedly his best friends—were to stand guard at the cave entrance.

Semicolons

Semicolons add creativity to sentence structure. They are usually used to link independent clauses (clauses that most likely can stand alone as a sentence) that are not joined by a coordinating conjunction (and, but, or, nor, for, so, or yet). Only use a semicolon between independent clauses that are closely related in meaning.

Example:
She seemed a little old-fashioned; I noticed that her shirt was out of style and her faded jeans flared at the knees.

Be careful with conjunctive adverbs, which always require a semicolon. Some conjunctive adverbs include: likewise, consequently, so, thus, moreover, indeed, afterwards, nevertheless, however, and therefore. See page 13 for a complete list of conjunctive adverbs.

Example:
Jane knew that she was overweight; nevertheless, she ate two banana splits for dessert.
Alex was saving money for college; thus, she worked two jobs.

- Semicolons separate items in a list that are long and complex or that include internal punctuation.

Example:
Where were you on the nights of December 28, 2008; December 31, 2008; and January 2, 2009?

Colons

Colons direct the reader's attention to what follows, whether it is a list or a phrase. They add: Emphasis!

Examples:
Listen carefully: your teacher will not accept late homework.
The grocery list read as follows: milk, butter, eggs, and bread.

Ellipsis

The **ellipsis** is a unique part of the punctuation arsenal and, if used sparingly, is effective and dramatic punctuation. The ellipse is three dots with a space between each dot.

Example:

The freezer is cold . . . very, very cold.

• The ellipsis can be used to indicate a list is much longer than words can express.

Example:

The shopping list this week was produce, paper products, office equipment . . . the list goes on . . . . *Note:* The fourth . at the end of the example here is a period.

• The ellipsis is used in place of words left out of a quotation.

Example:

(Abbreviated sentence)
Patrick Henry said, "Give me liberty or . . . death."
(Original sentence)
Patrick Henry said, "Give me liberty or give me death."

PARALLEL STRUCTURE

Parallel structure balances two or more similar words, phrases, or clauses to add smoothness and clarity to a sentence.

Example: I like to run, to ski, and to dance.

Example: I like running, skiing, and dancing.

Example: Lucky Charms features yellow stars, purple horseshoes, and red balloons.

Keep Lists Parallel

When you make a list, be sure each item in it has basically the same structure. The term for having a similar structure is **parallelism**.

Don't Write:	Do Write:
A typical business report has these preliminary elements:	A typical business report has these preliminary elements:
a cover page	a cover page
a table of contents	a table of contents
it also has an executive summary	an executive summary

PRONOUN AGREEMENT

Singular pronouns: him, her, he, she, it, anyone, anything, each, either, everyone, everything, neither, no one, nothing, what, whatever, whoever. These use singular verbs.

Plural pronouns: they, them, those, these, few, people, both, the rest. These use plural verbs.

Collective nouns: audience, class, group, gang, crowd, troupe. These use singular verbs.

RULES (AGAIN)

You may, or may not, agree with some "rules" that apply to business writing, but awareness of them is a sign of your professionalism. Recall that the point of this chapter is to make you aware of the things that comprise professional correspondence.

Sometimes rules are meant to be broken, or they are simply outdated. For example, the classical "rule" never to start a sentence with "and" or "but" went out in the 1960s. Today, rulebooks permit it, professional writers do it, it has rhetorical value, and it makes sense.

Nonetheless, there are other "rules" that define standard and "good" business writing; and protocol requires you to adhere to them. When in doubt, it is wise to err on the side of conformity—especially when the writing isn't really your own, but that of the company you represent.

In many ways, the idea of getting beyond the "rules" involves getting beyond your eighth grade. Those rules made little sense then, and yet there is more to them than we wanted to admit. The following are a few basic rules that will help to make your business correspondence accurate. That alone should make you feel better—besides, I think these guidelines explain the reasoning behind the rules better than those given back then "when we should have learned these things." Take them for what they are and make them part of your everyday correspondence. Sorry . . . that's just the way it is.

Split Infinitive

An infinitive is the word *to* followed by a verb form: to be, to find, to dance. **Split infinitives** put a modifier, often an adverb, between the word *to* and the verb form,

Example: to always be, to never find

To correct a split infinitive, put the modifier before or after the infinitive (the "to" verb).

Example:

> *Wrong (split infinitive):* For her to always arrive on time seems unrealistic.
> *Correct (unsplit infinitive):* For her always to arrive on time seems unrealistic.

Example:

> *Wrong (split infinitive):* I intended to properly understand computer programming.
> *Correct (unsplit infinitive):* I intended to understand computer programming properly.
> *Unsplit infinitive sentence:* She plans to be available and never to find a problem with the schedule.

Note: Even if you neither know nor care what a split infinitive is, the right place to be on the issue is knowing how to distinguish between the two types of infinitive structures.

Comma Splices and Fused Sentences

Comma splices and fused sentences are easy to identify. These are serious punctuation errors. A comma splice happens when you join two sentences with only a comma.

Examples:

> We worked over the weekend, we managed to accomplish many things.
> The radio is too loud, the static is overbearing.

You can fix comma splices by changing the comma to almost any other mark of punctuation, such as:

> a semicolon
> a dash
> a period

Examples:

> We worked over the weekend; we managed to accomplish many things.
> We worked over the weekend—we managed to accomplish many things.
> We worked over the weekend. We managed to accomplish many things.

Or, you can add a coordinating conjunction—like, and, or, so—after the comma.

Examples:

> We worked over the weekend, and we managed to accomplish many things.
> We worked over the weekend, so we managed to accomplish many things.

Coordinating Conjunctions

Coordinating conjunctions are joiners and can be used to "splice" together thoughts.

Coordinating conjunctions are used to fix comma splices:

and	nor	for
or	so	yet
but		

Just to confuse the issue . . . some words appear to be, but are *not*, coordinating conjunctions. They are, instead, **conjunctive adverbs** and cannot be used after a comma splice.

Conjunctive adverbs are used to fix comma splices:

accordingly	however	nevertheless
as a result	indeed	next
consequently	in fact	otherwise
first	instead	still
for example	likewise	therefore
furthermore	moreover	unfortunately

To use conjunctive adverbs, you need more sophisticated punctuation (semicolon, dash, etc.).

Examples:

> We worked over the weekend; therefore, we managed to accomplish many things.
> We worked over the weekend. Therefore, we managed to accomplish many things.
> We worked over the weekend. We did, therefore, manage to accomplish many things.

Fused Sentence

A **fused sentence** is simply a comma splice without the comma and is always wrong. In other words, the punctuation is missing.

You fix fused sentences the same way you fix comma splices: add punctuation (semicolon, dash, period) or add a comma and a coordinating conjunction (such as and, or, but).

Examples:

> *(Fused sentence):* The radio is too loud the static is overbearing.
> *(Corrected fused sentence):* The radio is too loud; therefore, the static is overbearing.
> The radio is too loud. Therefore, the static is overbearing.
> The radio is too loud: the static, therefore, is overbearing.
> The radio is too loud. The static is overbearing.

Editing Tips

- Identify your audience, then choose an appropriate tone for your letter.

- Use an outline. It can help you realize what you want to accomplish in a piece of writing.

- Analyze the sentences in each paragraph of the writing: what does each sentence do and what does it say? In other words, what is its purpose and what does it accomplish? Write with clarity.

- Read your finished piece of writing aloud to yourself slowly. This way you can hear mistakes in the writing. Put the writing away for an evening before you do this. The longer you are away from it, the better you will be at catching typos and grammatical mistakes.

- When writing a memo, be careful about using the word *you* when *one* is meant.

Example:

Informal: The restaurant was so good that it made you want to eat all the food!
Formal: The restaurant was so good that it made the patron (or one) want to eat all the food!

- Do not use *their* or *they* for gender-neutral, singular pronouns.

Example:

Incorrect: The winner may claim their prize at the ticket booth. They are lucky!
Correct: The winner may claim his or her prize at the ticket booth. He or she is lucky! Passive voice can also be used to get around this: The prize may be picked up at the ticket booth by the lucky winner.

- Do not use *myself* in place of *me* or *I*; don't use *I* where *me* should be.

Example:

Incorrect: Dan met with myself and Ally. Dan met with Ally and I.
Correct: Dan met with Ally and me.

How can you check to make sure you've chosen correctly? Take the other person's name out of the sentence. Which is correct? Dan met with I or Dan met with me?

- Punctuation always goes INSIDE quotation marks.

Example: Pete said "She left already."

Chapter Questions and Exercises

1. Passive–Active Voice Exercise:
   Change the following sentences from passive to active voice.
   a. A gun was lifted, a step was taken forward, and he tumbled down the stairs, cursing.
   b. It is recommended that the position be filled by a woman.
   c. The constitution was completely rewritten by the board of directors.

2. Punctuation Exercise:
   Add correct punctuation where necessary. Not all sentences need punctuation. Some need more than one punctuation mark.
   a. The two men quickly bolted the door but the intruder had already entered through the window.
   b. Before penicillin and other antibiotics were developed pneumonia was fatal.
   c. Penn State after all is a world-class university.
   d. The canned goods beans, potatoes, and peas were in the back seat.
   e. Three vegetables have an undeserved reputation for being fattening potatoes asparagus and summer squash.
   f. Climbing can be a dangerous hobby consequently one should never go climbing alone.
   g. "No" Mark said "I don't want to go."
   h. The Nittany Lion Penn State's mascot is a familiar feature at many sporting events.
   i. I want you to remember one thing I did not steal your car.
   j. Yes times have changed.
   k. The coach can't play the game she can only instruct and encourage.
   l. The man wearing the white rose is the bridegroom
   m. You have therefore no reason to leave town.
   n. The second robber who served as lookout got away.
   o. The festival will open with the following films *Reservoir Dogs* and *Pulp Fiction*.

3. Parallel Structure Exercise:
   Revise the following sentences to contain parallel structure.
   a. College students are too often influenced by the desires of their parents, grades, and their friends.
   b. He was a good provider, a good husband, and he was also a good friend.
   c. Alice is interested in many professions such as medicine, being a teacher, and journalism.

4. Pronoun Agreement Exercise:
   Complete the following sentences with the correct form of the verb in parentheses.
   a. The class (look) to the teacher for guidance.
   b. Anyone who (wish) to attend may buy tickets at the Eisenhower Box Office.
   c. Neither Jeff nor Jessica (want) to go to the party.
   d. The first two problems are difficult, but the rest (be) easy.
   e. Either of these buses (go) past the university.

   Revise the following sentences to make them more understandable.
   a. My neighbor serves beets to her kids, but she doesn't like them.
   b. Jane asked Mrs. Simon about her father's illness, which led to an awkward silence.

5. What is wrong with the following sentences?
   a. I hope we meet in an accident very soon.
   b. You make my heart sour.
   c. Where do I place the coma in the sentence?
   d. I have to pee my money.

    e. The waiter is cold and wet and a little windy.

    f. We hired an inferior decorator to remodel the dinner.

    g. Our dinner guest started joking on her food.

    h. She wants to order a sammich.

    i. Carol's arm has been breaking for six weeks.

    j. The chef makes all the food from scratching.

    k. Mushrooms are starting to grow in me.

    l. Don't forget to insult the cook.

    m. The groom was wearing a very nice croissant.

    n. He lifted the veal off her face and gave her a big kiss.

    o. This marriage has ended: go in Peace.

6. Visit a local restaurant, cafe, or fast-food chain. Observe the food, atmosphere, and the service. Write a review in a voice that matches the style of the restaurant.

Key Terms

- Style
- Voice
- Tone
- Clarity
- Passive voice

- Active voice
- Dashes
- Semicolons
- Colons
- Ellipsis

- Parallelism
- Split infinitive
- Coordinating conjunctions
- Conjunctive adverbs
- Fused sentence

Helpful Websites:

http://englishplus.com/grammar/

http://www.webgrammar.com/

2 ADMINISTRATION

Juanita Qu works in the corporate office for RSVP Services, a busy, medium-sized event planning company in San Diego, California. RSVP provides event planning, event management, event marketing, meeting planning, and conference planning. No event is too big, or too small. Services provided by RSVP include catering, entertainment, and transportation. Depending upon the time of year, RSVP is more or less busy... and frequently, RSVP has up to 600 employees on the roster, many of whom are part-time, temporary, or seasonal.

As an administrator for RSVP, Juanita faces each day—practically each minute of each day—as an ever-changing event in itself. She is the master at the helm. Everyone who works for RSVP depends upon her to "get it right." Juanita prides herself on providing administrative "clear sailing" for all those associated with the company.

Juanita's rolodex is massive. She knows who can provide what services: build stages, transport people, entertain, arrange flowers, cater large and small groups, create signage, and so on. There is no end to what Juanita has been asked to provide for RSVP, and she has yet to hear it all.

As a key administrator, Juanita writes all the time. Her correspondence runs the gamut—from high praise to criticism. Above all, Juanita is always professional, even when she is disappointed and compelled to complain.

Introduction

This chapter deals with various documents that originate in the administrative offices of a hospitality operation. For example, you might be called on to formulate reports, documents, memos, abstracts, summaries, business letters... the list goes on. It is widely assumed that anyone working in the administrative office knows how to keep files, field phone calls, and do the writing required. We all know, however, that is not always the case. Before going any further, a word of advice: review and edit each and every document that goes out with your name on it. Few things are more embarrassing than signing off on a letter with typos or improper formatting. And if you write for someone else, your credibility is on the line to write properly.

EFFECTIVE WRITING REQUIRES SOME SPECIFIC STEPS

Step 1 Identify the audience
Step 2 Organize the message
Step 3 Select the medium
Step 4 Write the draft
Step 5 Review and revise

Identify the Audience

Administrators write to different people: customers, employees, supervisors, colleagues, and purveyors. Although you will have your own style, you may want to approach different audiences with different tones. Chapter 1, the grammar chapter, explained style and tone, so we will not go into those topics again here. The point of identifying your audience is to help your readers understand what it is you want to say.

Who, exactly, will read your document? Will it have many readers, or is it confidential? What are your needs? What are the needs of the reader(s)? Do you need to inject humor, or display confidence? Are you asking for suggestions, or is this a directive aimed at subordinates?

In identifying your audience, you will also decide what it is, exactly, that you want to say.

Organize the Message

Organization is the cornerstone of any successful writing project. Although the process may seem tedious, outlining always helps in organizing the points to be covered. Outlines don't necessarily need to be long and detailed. Index cards, for example, are quick, easy tools to use in outlining. An outline can also be bullet points, or it can be multilayered.

The main idea behind organizing your message is to develop it sequentially. This is particularly relevant when giving instructions or directions. Imagine that you are driving in a new city and that you are lost. You stop to ask for directions. Do you want someone to start at where you are now and then explain step-by-step how to get where you want to go? Or do you want someone to begin with where you are going and then explain how to get there? Either of these sequences can be effective, but the organization of the directions will differ.

Select the Medium

There are a variety of mediums for sending written messages. You can choose from letters, memos, e-mail, fax, and handwritten notes.

Ask yourself: What is the most appropriate way to get my message across? Today's electronic technologies enable written communication ... but perhaps a printed letter is more appropriate. Though rarely used, using pen and ink is a most effective way to write a thank-you. In some instances, you may elect to send both an electronic message with an attachment and a follow-up handwritten, signed note.

Letters

Your company should have letterhead stationery; if it doesn't, order some. When using it, you should also affix your business card with a paper clip to the upper right or left side of the paper. The quality of stationery and the paper is important when writing, for it sends a subtle message about you.

Memos

Memos are generally used for internal communication among members of the same organization. They have a variety of purposes, but the overarching idea is communality.

E-mail

E-mail is ubiquitous. In fact, e-mail correspondence is often the preferred means of business communication. And it will probably become more universal, if you can imagine, as larger percentages of the global population become computer savvy.

The advantages of e-mail are mainly that it is quicker and less expensive than ground mail. Recall that it wasn't until e-mail that the term "snail mail" became synonymous with the postal service. As beautiful and seamless as e-mail seems, however, there are some serious concerns in using it.

The main problem with e-mail is that once the "send" button is pressed, it is on its way. Technology exists to recall an e-mail, but one must be quick and there is always the risk that someone, somewhere saw it. The following sample shows how one message, sent two different ways, are very different.

E-MAIL FAUX PAS—WHAT HAPPENS WITH THE PUSH OF A BUTTON

Erin meant to send e-mail #2 to her relatives. . . but she mistakenly sent e-mail #1 first. Note misspellings, omissions of words, and incorrect capitalization. This is an "Oops!" message.

E-MAIL #1—SENT TO MOM, DAD, AUNTS, UNCLES, AND GRANDMA, BUT INTENDED FOR FRIENDS:

Hey Pitt pallys and home slices,

IRELAND IS FAN F***ING TASTIC. I got here three days ago and everything is amazing. My friends are really cool, there is no one here like you all. I swear, but I feel like I am going to have such a good time. I am living in the best part of Dublin and our apartment is sweet. My roomates seem really nice and cool and if anyone plans on visiting (which you better) they said it's totally cool if you want to stay here instead of having to get a hotel. I would love to have ppl come over. The atmosphere is amazing and the people are just soooo nice. I already met some old retired couple who invited me to stay at their house some weekend. My classes are going to be amazing and the beer here is great. I have been drunk every night. The first thing I did was have a guiness in honor of you all. Tonight I am going to a pub crawl and its gonna be insanity. We are going to Temple Bar, which is the coolest spot in town. My friends are totally down with drinking and we are gonna travel too. Its so weird to not be at Pitt with y'all. I do have pangs of being homesick, but mostly I am too excited and too busy to think about that stuff. I am def. going to Amsterdam, Prague and italy. . . . rachael, when are you gonna be in Siena til? I wanna visit sooo bad! Alright, there is a lot more to say, but I already sent a huge e-mail and it got erased. . . I was soooo pissed. Write back and tell me how you are all doing and what the semester is like. I want to hear all about whats going on with everyone. I thought a mass e-mail would be the best way to start things and I will write back to whoever responds. Its cool if you don't. . . I know how busy and hectic everything is right now for everyone. I love you all and I miss you. There is so much more to say, but I am hogging the computer and I need to get ready for going out tonight. love you all so much!

Much Love,
Biddle!

(*continued*)

E-MAIL #2—SENT TO FRIENDS BUT INTENDED FOR FAMILY: AUNTS, UNCLES, AND GRANDMA

Subject: Greetings from Ireland
Date: Fri, 23 Jan 2004 18:25:01 -0500

Hello family and friends,

Greetings from the Emerald Isle. Everything over is still wonderful, but time seems to be going by so fast already. My apartment is wonderful and I love my roomates. I moved last week because my old roommate was a light sleeper and apparently I snored. So now I am in a new house, and I love it. I live with three girls and two boys and I love them all. We frequently have "family dinners" and go out together. Last weekend I went to County Cork with four of my friends. We toured the Blarney Castle, drank Guinness, saw some live Celtic music, and then went to Killarney National Park and biked through that all day. We biked about six hours and saw in the park a 15th Century Abbey, a castle, a beautiful waterfall, and tons of amazing scenery. I took so many pictures, I can't wait for everyone to see them. I am in love with Ireland, I never want to come back. I have been going to the theater quite a bit, and last week I actually saw a play about! rugby. I didn't really understand it at first, but it ended up being really funny once I understood their accents. Tomorrow we are going to the Gate Theater downtown to see Jane Eyre. There is so much to do and see just in Dublin I occasionally get overwhelmed. I try to see one museum a week. This week's choice was the National Museum where I saw the Tara Brooch and lots of old Celtic jewelry. Tomorrow we are also doing the literary pub crawl through Temple Bar area. I so excited for that. How is everything in the States. I try to read the papers and keep up but sometimes it's difficult over here because I am so busy. Classes seem to be going well although I have lots to read. I really love my Irish theater and social change class and my mythmaking and nationalism class. For spring break my theater class is going to London for the weekend and seeing many shows in the West End. I am also planning on going to Edinburgh, Amsterdam, Prague and Rome while here. Alright, just wanted to send out an update on how everything is over here. I am absolutely loving every day. Hope you are doing well. Send me e-mails and tell me how you are all doing.

Love,
Erin

Fax

It's difficult to imagine the business world without the fax machine, yet it has been around only a little more than 25 years. Faxes are great when speed is essential, particularly if a contract, diagram, or illustration is involved. Another reason to choose a fax for business correspondence is if a signature, initial, or change in writing is required. For example, a real estate deal may require initials and changes that need to be transmitted immediately. The fax is an ideal way to do this.

Sometimes people have their own private fax machines, but usually the faxed message can be viewed easily by someone else. Offices typically have one fax number that is shared by a number of people. I have received faxes meant for someone else entirely (whom I didn't know). It is important to remember that if the material is sensitive, not to use a fax machine.

Write the First Draft

Expect to write more than one draft of your letter, memo, document, or report. You might start with the easiest part, but remember to write to your audience. You may type directly into your computer or handwrite it first using pencil and paper. I frequently start my first draft with pencil and index cards, though this usually turns into an outline.

The first draft is just that—don't become frustrated if it doesn't sound exactly as you want it to sound. Ask yourself: What exactly do I want to say? Whom am I talking to? If you have time, have someone else read your writing or—weird as it may sound—read it aloud to yourself. You will be amazed at how many mistakes you catch simply by reading aloud.

Topic Sentence

Is your topic sentence or main idea clearly stated? The topic sentence is usually the first sentence of a paragraph, and each sentence within that paragraph follows up the idea. New paragraphs unfold from that idea.

Use of Paragraphs

Paragraphs exist to keep ideas together. A general rule is three sentences to each paragraph, but this rule can also be broken. Too many short and choppy paragraphs give the impression of not being certain of the message.

Transitions

Making transitions between thoughts is important. Transitions can be obvious or they can be subtle.

Example:
Obvious transition
Having reached the five-star level, we are now ready to focus on staying there.

Subtle transition
Even though we have reached the five-star level, we remain concerned about staying there.

Headings or bold type can help to establish the flow of the document and can serve as transitions from one point to the next. The main question to ask yourself is: Are my transitions effective?

Review and Revise

Rarely is a good letter or, for that matter, any piece of writing in final form after the first draft. If you have time, set it aside for a bit . . . then come back and read it again for clarity of purpose and tone. Again, have someone review your writing. Ask him or her to make constructive comments and raise questions, and don't get defensive or feel insulted when questioned about your meaning.

You might also consult a thesaurus to find a better way to say what you want to say. It should be noted, however, that "plain" vocabulary is far more effective than "showy" vocabulary, particularly if the words used don't match the way you would normally speak.

BUSINESS LETTERS

Much correspondence is in the form of a letter. For example, letters are used to communicate praise, complaints, an apology for poor service, a demand for payment, inquiries, and refusals. While each type of letter is idiosyncratic, their basic formats are similar.

Most companies have their own formats for business letters, and these should always be adhered to when using official stationery. This book presents two types of business letter that are generally accepted in any office environment: Block style and Modified Semi-block style. However, there are several variations to these styles. A good secretarial handbook, which should be on hand in any administrative office, will include examples of these variations.

Assuming that you have company stationery, five essential elements of any business letter are: *date line, inside address, salutation, message,* and *closing with signature.* Each is discussed below. The samples provided show the basic layout and format for a typical business letter and the placement of specific information.

Main Parts

Date Line

The date line appears two to six lines below the letterhead, approximately one inch from the top of the page. The full date—not abbreviated, but completely spelled out—appears on this line (for example, January 1, 2xxx). The date line may be flush left, centered, or just right of center. Companies will usually specify their preference for the placement of the date line.

Inside Address

The inside address usually includes the name(s), title, company name, street address, and city of the person to whom the letter is written. Other information, such as department or building, may also be included and is placed between the title and the company name. See samples of inside addresses for variations. A good idea is to follow the style used on the business card of the person receiving the letter or search on the Internet for an official presentation.

The inside address is placed three lines below the date. It is always single-spaced and is usually flush with the left margin. Always check the official spelling and punctuation and use of abbreviations for a company and title abbreviations for use in the inside address.

Salutation

The salutation is placed two lines beneath the last line of the inside address. The salutation is followed by a colon in business correspondence; the comma is reserved for personal correspondence. Do not use the full name in the salutation (as you did in the inside address). At this point, use the title.

Dear Mr. Brown:
Dear Dr. Brown:
Dear Ms. Brown:

If possible, avoid using impersonal salutations such as "To Whom It May Concern" or "Dear Sir or Madam." Admittedly, there are times when it is impossible to address each letter individually, but whenever possible try to be creative. For example, you might write "Dear Esteemed Guest" or "Dear Students." Nonetheless, the use of a personal salutation always demonstrates your effort to reach your reader.

Message

The message is the body of the letter. It begins two spaces below the salutation. The message should contain paragraphs of at least three sentences with a double space between each paragraph. Rarely is the text of a letter double-spaced, particularly in business correspondence.

Most business letters are formatted in Block style or Modified Semi-block style. The samples provided show the differences between the two. If a letter extends to two or more pages, at least three lines should appear on the last page plus the signature. Do not post a letter with only the signature on the last page. The second (and all additional pages) of a letter should follow the same pattern as the first, that is, a one-inch margin at the top of the letter before beginning the text. You should identify the continuation sheet with a heading that includes the page number, date, and name of recipient.

Closing

The closing is typed two lines below the last line of the message. The placement of the closing is determined by the style being used. For example, Block format places the closing flush with the left margin; a Modified Semi-block style places the closing just right of dead center.

Four spaces are left between the complimentary close and the typed name of the sender to be used for an inked signature. Blue ink is considered more appropriate in business writing than black ink.

COMPLIMENTARY CLOSING FOR LETTERS

Formal: Respectfully	Informal: Cordially	Informal: Best regards
Polite: Very truly yours	Friendly: Best wishes	European: Yours faithfully
Friendly: Sincerely		

Extras

Identification Initials

The initials of the typist (usually three are used) appear two lines below the last line of the signature. They are aligned flush left in all letter styles. Some variations, for example, indicating who typed the letter for whom, are used; the preference is determined by the company.

Enclosure(s)

Many letters are accompanied by one or more enclosures. This information follows the typist's initials and is separated from them by one or two blank lines. Variations on this theme include:

Enclosure: map
Enclosures: (3)
Enclosures: map, directions

Carbon Copy

Though the days of the carbon copy have passed, the use of c.c. or b.c.c. is still with us. In fact, these initials are part of many e-mail headings. Courtesy copy, c.c., is used to alert the receiver that a copy was sent to the other individuals named; b.c.c., meaning blind courtesy copy, indicates the receiver was not alerted that someone else received a copy.

The c.c. is placed one or two lines after the previous, which could be the enclosure line, the typist's initials, or the signature line. The name(s) of those copied on the document are always spelled out. Other information can include the title or addresses.

Note: Do not underestimate the effectiveness of the carbon copy. The c.c. is a very powerful tool that ensures others see the same document. It acts in many ways as verification. It also often requires a letter to be discussed by the receivers.

SAMPLE BLOCK STYLE LETTER

Company Logo
Address
Web site

May 1, 2xxx

Philip E. Smith, Executive Director
Marketing Department
ABC Company
4321 Executive Blvd.
Anytown, ST 90080

Dear Mr. Smith:

This is a Block letter. Note that all the paragraphs are flush left. The margins are one inch on either side. The sentences are single spaced. There are double spaces between the paragraphs. The date line is typed between two and six lines beneath the company letterhead logo, which includes the return address. Usually, three sentences are included in each paragraph. The content of each paragraph should contain connected thoughts.

The inside address should be three lines below the date, which is two or three lines below the company logo and address. Although this can vary, one inch below is a good starting point for the date. The salutation contains a formal "Mr.," "Ms.," or "Dr." followed by the last name. Colons always follow the salutation in business writing—never use a comma.

The message starts flush left, two lines after the salutation. Use single spacing for the message and a double space between paragraphs. Second or third pages should have at least three lines of the message on the page. A heading for these pages that synchronizes with the cover page includes the page number, date, and name of the recipient.

The last paragraph should include information that serves as a "wrap-up." You can thank the person for his or her consideration, suggest an action to be taken, provide a time and date for the next meeting or phone call, etc. The idea is to provide information for taking action that the correspondence will require.

The complimentary close is typed two lines below the last sentence in the message. Four blank lines are required for a signature. The letter should be signed in blue ink. The title of the writer can appear below the typed signature.

Extra information can follow the signature of the writer: typist's initials, enclosure(s), and names of those receiving courtesy copies. Finally, written letters serve as documentation of an event and should always be reviewed for spelling, grammar, and punctuation errors.

Most respectfully yours,

Donna Lincoln --- who this letter is from
Consultant --- business of title
Blv --- who typed this letter

Enclosures: Map
            Directions

cc Valerie Morgan, Esq.

SAMPLE MODIFIED SEMI-BLOCK STYLE

Company Logo
Address
Web site

May 1, 2xxx

Philip E. Smith, Executive Director
Marketing Department
ABC Company
4321 Executive Blvd.
Anytown, ST 90080

Dear Mr. Smith:

This is a Modified Semi-block style letter. One difference from the Block style is that the date is placed either in the center or just right of the center. As in the Block style, the inside address is flush left. Another difference is that the paragraphs are indented five (5) spaces. Another version of the Modified Semi-block style indents the paragraphs ten (10) spaces, though this is not very common, except in memos (see memo sample).

Another distinct difference in the Modified Semi-block style is the complimentary close and the signature. They are aligned with the date; that is, they are also indented just right of center. Make sure that the date and the signature align correctly. Not aligning them exactly creates a visual mess and makes the overall letter askew. Otherwise, the spacing and style of the close and signature are the same: two lines below the message for the complimentary close, four lines of space below for the typed signature, the business title to follow, and the signature to be signed in blue ink.

The other components of the Modified Semi-block style are the same as the Block style. The paragraphs are single-spaced with double spaces between each paragraph. The typist's initials and indications for enclosures and courtesy copies are flush left as in the Block style.

Sincerely,

Enid Nicely
Business Title

Blv
Enclosures: (2)
cc Valerie Morgan, Esq.

POSTSCRIPT

A postscript (or P.S.) follows two to four lines below the last notation in any letter. If a Block style is used, then position the P.S. flush left. If a Modified Semi-block style is used, then indent the P.S. five spaces. Any postscript should be initialed by the writer.

MEMOS

Memorandums, or memos, have a specific format and design. Any memo should contain the information necessary to identify the person(s) receiving the memo, the author of the memo, the person who wrote the memo (who can be someone other than the author), the date, and the subject. The samples provided show the basic format for a memo and the placement of specific information.

Main Parts
Heading
The heading contains the guide words *To*, *From*, *Date*, and *Subject*. These guide words are placed at the top, left-hand side of the document. Guide words are followed by a colon and are aligned two spaces after the longest word (usually, *Subject*). See the samples provided.

> *To* identifies the person(s) or group receiving the memo. The department(s) associated with the person(s) may follow on a second line. If more than one person is receiving the memo, a check mark is placed next to each person's name. *From* identifies the author(s). The department associated with the author may follow on a second line.

SAMPLE INTEROFFICE MEMORANDUM

TO: Margaret Smith
             Food & Beverage Department

FROM: Kelly North
             Personnel Department

DATE: Month, Day, 2xxx

SUBJECT: Company format for writing an interoffice memo

Margins at the top and side of the document should be at least one inch. Guide words are aligned at the left margin. You may choose to use a ten-space tab for the message.

Two or three blank lines appear after the SUBJECT. You can choose to use the Block paragraph style, in which all paragraphs begin flush left, or you can indent all paragraphs ten spaces to align with the heading. Either is acceptable.

Two blank lines appear after the body of the memo. The author's initials are typed beneath the last line of the last paragraph. They appear just to the right of center.

K.N.

lcc *(this is the typist)*

cc Abigail Raemont *(these are the full names of the two other recipients for this memo)*
Alex Biddle

Date: The full date—not abbreviated, but completely spelled out—appears on this line.

Subject: A brief description of the general idea is written in the subject line.

Body

Leave two or three blank lines before beginning the body of the message. Various formats are acceptable; typically, paragraphs are typed in Block style (with no indentions for the paragraphs) or indented five or ten spaces. See the samples provided.

Closing

Two or three lines follow the main body of the memo and the writer's initials are typed just right of the center. The author of the memo should initial, in ink, either next to the typed initials or at the heading next to his or her name. This ensures that the memo is official and has been reviewed by the writer.

Frequently, administrative assistants type a memo, and his or her initials should also appear in the closing. The typist's initials, enclosure(s) notation, and carbon copy notations appear on the bottom left side.

ENVELOPES

Believe it or not, somewhere along the way someone formulated an "official" way to address an envelope. The idea behind envelopes reminds me of a story about an exchange student from Argentina, Gaby Valoschin, who stayed with us for one year. To my amazement, Gaby had never addressed an envelope in her 17 years. She was faced with this dilemma when sending a letter to her mother. Gaby explained that Argentinians never used the post to mail items, unbelievable as that sounds. I immediately found it necessary to whip out my samples of "how to address an envelope." Gaby was duly impressed—first, that there was a formality to addressing an envelope and, second, that I actually had a file on envelopes in my office.

The following information is essential in addressing an envelope. This book does not go into the protocol for titles, but you should know that they exist. A properly addressed envelope is shown in the sample.

Notes on Addressing an Envelope

1. The addressees' full names and geographical addresses are typed vertically and horizontally in the center.
2. All special mailing notations are placed below the stamp.
3. The sender's full name and geographical address are printed or typed in the upper left corner.
4. The address should be clear and understandable.
5. If typed, the address should take no more than 1½" × ¾" of space. A of space of ⅝" should be left at the bottom edge of the envelope.
6. Any address with four or more lines should be single spaced.
7. An address with three lines can be double-spaced.
8. There are standard postal codes for each country and its dependencies.
9. Etiquette dictates the proper way to address persons on an envelope.

STATE ABBREVIATIONS

STATE/POSSESSION	ABBREVIATION	STATE/POSSESSION	ABBREVIATION
Alabama	AL	Montana	MT
Alaska	AK	Nebraska	NE
American Samoa	AS	Nevada	NV
Arizona	AZ	New Hampshire	NH
Arkansas	AR	New Jersey	NJ
California	CA	New Mexico	NM
Colorado	CO	New York	NY
Connecticut	CT	North Carolina	NC
Delaware	DE	North Dakota	ND
District of Columbia	DC	Northern Mariana	MP
Federated States of	FM	Islands	
Micronesia		Ohio	OH
Florida	FL	Oklahoma	OK
Georgia	GA	Oregon	OR
Guam	GU	Palau	PW
Hawaii	HI	Pennsylvania	PA
Idaho	ID	Puerto Rico	PR
Illinois	IL	Rhode Island	RI
Indiana	IN	South Carolina	SC
Iowa	IA	South Dakota	SD
Kansas	KS	Tennessee	TN
Kentucky	KY	Texas	TX
Louisiana	LA	Utah	UT
Maine	ME	Vermont	VT
Marshall Islands	MH	Virgin Islands	VI
Maryland	MD	Virginia	VA
Massachusetts	MA	Washington	WA
Michigan	MI	West Virginia	WV
Minnesota	MN	Wisconsin	WI
Mississippi	MS	Wyoming	WY
Missouri	MO		

SOURCE: http://www.usps.com/ncsc/lookups/usps_abbreviations.html

BROCHURES

There are two types of brochures: **informational brochures** and **sales brochures**. Either requires the ability to persuade, and by means of all available media: text, photos, how-to information, and contacts. The first questions to ask are: What is this brochure meant to do? Who is my audience?

Informational Brochures

Informational brochures are designed to convey a certain image of your company. They must cover who, what, where, when, and how. What is the information you want to give people? Do you have a specific, targeted audience, or is your audience general? What is the message? What look do you want? Do you want a "hip" look, or do you want to appeal to an audience that is more conservative? All of this is expressed in the style of writing and the photos used. Fortunately, there are media companies available to help you work through these conundrums, and if you are about to spend monies on a brochure, it is highly recommended you connect with one of these specialized companies to help you get your message across.

Either way, when setting out to design a brochure for your company, you want to have a target in mind. This requires a meeting of the minds. Designing a brochure is not a job for one person, and you should plan on months of regularly scheduled meetings before seeing the brochure in print. Furthermore, after the printed copy is in hand, you need to get it out there. There is nothing worse than having paid for thousands of copies of a brochure only to have it sit in boxes in the warehouse or, worse still, your office.

Sales Brochures

Sales brochures are created to sell your company's products and services and should be targeted. The main idea with a sales brochure is to grab the attention of the audience. Who is your audience? Is there a new product to be highlighted? A picture identifying the product should be prominently displayed on the front cover along with only minimal text. Too many words will not do; they should be reserved for the inside panels of the brochure. Contact information must be prominently displayed in more than one place—perhaps on both the front and the back panels.

With any brochure, the layout and design are crucial. Should your brochure be small and easily tucked into a coat pocket? Do you want a one-page flyer? Is it an all-out, four-color, eight-page project? (Note that brochures are printed in four-page segments.) How do you want to present yourself? How much can you afford?

Always copyright your brochures, and make sure all of the information included is your own or, if it is borrowed from another source, that you have permission to use it. A publishing contract should cover who is responsible for any typos that might occur. Have many people review the brochure before the final press run is made.

We often get caught up in and too close to our own media work. Have all the bases been covered? Has any group been missed? Will anyone be offended? The more eyes that see a brochure before it goes out, the more feedback you get . . . particularly negative. This is good information. Don't be shortsighted and think that any one person can put together a succesful brochure; it's always a group effort.

REPORTS

Administrators in most business frequently find themselves responsible for writing reports. Hospitality organizations are no different. Typical reports include feasibility reports and proposals, progress and activity reports, accident reports, and trip reports. Each of these reports has a specific purpose and desired outcome.

All reports contain an **introduction**, a **body**, a **conclusion**, and a **recommendation**. The recommendation could include an **action plan** for follow-up (such as in an accident report or trip report). Each of these sections for a report is discussed briefly next.

The **introduction** states the intent or purpose of the report and gives a description of the situation and background information. The idea is to provide an overview of what will be contained in the report.

The **body** presents the details. If the report is lengthy, the body may be broken into sections. Use subheadings when necessary to add to the clarity of the report.

The **conclusion** is a summary or synopsis of the report. It reviews what has already been said but also points out the most important ideas.

The **recommendation** includes points to be considered for the future. The author should have an opinion about what ideas, alternatives, or concepts will work best. Suggestions for improvements and changes and potential problems are described in this section. Recommendations might also include a suggested plan of action for the future.

Types of Reports

Feasibility Reports and Proposals

Feasibility reports are prepared before a project is undertaken. Consider it a survey to determine a project's likelihood of succeeding. Proposals in many ways are similar to feasibility reports, although proposals are more likely to take a sales pitch approach.

Progress and Activity Reports

Progress and activity reports serve to document ongoing activities. Progress reports are more often concerned with major projects in general, whereas activity reports are more specific. Each can be written on a regular basis. For example, if your company is opening a series of stores across a certain region, the area manager may provide both a progress report on the openings and an activity report on individuals involved in the project.

Accident Reports

Many companies have an official form to be completed should an accident occur, including injury on the job, equipment failure, employee health problems, or ill guests. Accident reports are crucial for documentation and should be completed as quickly as possible. Many managers must file an accident report before leaving for the day.

If there is no company form for accident reports, a memo is the best means of communicating what happened. It should include an overview or summary of the accident, any important details (note: minor information can be an important detail), and information about what action was taken. An action plan should also be included with the accident report to address procedures to be taken in the future to remedy the situation.

Trip Reports

Trip reports are required to document information about business trips. A trip report is frequently considered internal correspondence and so takes the form of a memo. It is addressed to an immediate supervisor and includes where the trip was made, who was visited, the purpose of the trip, the outcome of the meeting, and future implications for the company. Trip reports are used as documentation of employee development and successes and also document expenses for tax purposes.

EXECUTIVE SUMMARIES OR ABSTRACTS

The executive summary or abstract is a brief, comprehensive summary of a document, article, or proceeding, allowing readers to survey the contents quickly. It is like an outline of key points contained in a much longer piece of writing. When writing an executive summary or abstract, it is best to paraphrase rather than quote. Include the authors' names and the date of publication.

The best summaries do these things in the following order:

- Briefly summarize the purpose of the report or paper
- Summarize the specific nature of the work or assignment
- Provide basic information about the topic
- Point the reader towards the conclusion
- In general, executive summaries or abstracts are not a commentary and are straightforward and objective in tone
- Are efficient (no filler)
- Provide some condensed background information and an overview or purpose statement
- Cite the authors' names and dates
- Point out relationships among topics, especially via transition words
- Are written from an outline
- Use present-tense verbs
- Stick to the key ideas

To write a good executive summary or abstract:

Be accurate: Ensure that it reflects the purpose and content of the manuscript. Do not include information that does not appear in the body of the main article.

Make it self-contained: Do no use abbreviations and acronyms. Spell out all names and define unique terms.

Be concise and specific: Make each sentence maximally informative, especially the lead sentence. Be as brief as possible.

Be nonevaluative: Report rather than evaluate, do not add to or comment on what is in the body of the manuscript.

Make it coherent and readable: Write in clear and vigorous prose. Use verbs rather than the noun equivalents and the active rather than the passive voice.

PRESS RELEASES

Working with the press can result in free media exposure. The media include radio, television, the national, regional, and local press, and reviews. Oddly, mail is better than phone calls in making contact with the media, and proper formatting of your print material can help get their attention.

Getting media attention might require a press kit, a press release, a short note (possibly handwritten), or a business letter.

Press Kit

Your press kit should include some basics: fact sheet, biographies of the key players (chef, general manager, person in charge), the history of your property, menus, other press clips, graphics, and recipes. We will not detail each of these in this book; know that they all combine to present an image of your property and they all should be of high quality, including the paper and photography used and the written material.

Press Release

The press release has some basic components: *headline, contact information*, and a *story* or "hook." A well-written press release may be used as it stands in the publication to which it is sent. The editor may find the piece worthy enough to reprint without editing. This is the best situation, short of having a full-blown feature written about your story. Needless to say, there is nothing quite like "free" publicity that appears as what others think of you.

Headline

The headline should be direct and factual. The idea is to grab attention. Contact information should be placed at the top of the page. In a minimum number of words, the headline needs to say exactly what the story is. Read headlines in magazines and newspapers and mimic them. What is the news story? What is it that grabs the readers' attention? See the samples included here to get an idea of what is considered a "catch" or "hook" that will make the press person interested enough to call you for the full story.

Contact Information

Make it easy for the writer to contact you. Provide names, phone numbers, e-mail address, and fax numbers.

The "Hook"

Keep your release short and to the point. Include specific bits of information that are both important and newsworthy. What do the readers of that specific newspaper, trade publication, or magazine want to hear? The who write for various publications write for their constituency. What do you have to offer them?

- Keep your release short and to the point.
- Double-space your information.
- Staple if more than two pages.

- Overnight your information.
- Provide photos.

PRESS RELEASES: DOS AND DON'TS

Do

Read the publications and know who wants what information.

Think about the "hooks."

Create ideas.

Train your staff how to handle the press.

Send a thank-you note if an article appears about you.

Don't

Send gifts.

Be overly pushy.

Think you are owed a story.

Ways to Get Media Attention:

Press kit   Brief telephone call

Press release   Letter or e-mail

Short note

Chapter Questions and Exercises

Discuss the consequences of the following writing snags. Write an example of each point and correct it. The first one is done for you.

1. Beginning a letter with the salutation *Dear Gentlemen:*

   Example: DON'T WRITE: <u>Dear Gentlemen:</u>

   Reason: <u>The person to whom the letter is being sent may be a woman.</u>

   DO SAY: <u>Dear Sir or Madam:</u> (if you aren't sure and couldn't be bothered to find out to whom the letter is directed.) Better yet, <u>find out the name of the person</u> (a simple phone call should provide this) and confirm the spelling. Then address the correspondence personally—it's sure to have a bigger impact—for example: Dear Ms. Smyth.

2. Signing a letter with "Love."

   Example: DON'T WRITE: _____

   Reason: _____

   DO WRITE: _____

3. Verbosity, that is, going on, and on, and on.

   Example: DON'T WRITE: _____

   Reason: _____

   DO WRITE: _____

4. Use of obscenities and outbursts.

   Example: DON'T WRITE: _____

   Reason: _____

   DO WRITE: _____

5. Embarrassing familiarity.

   Example: DON'T WRITE: _____

   Reason: _____

   DO WRITE: _____

6. Lack of control.

   Example: DON'T WRITE: _____

   Reason: _____

   DO WRITE: _____

7. Define a good executive summary. Name five (5) key elements of an executive summary and explain the role that each plays.

8. Prepare a press release for your company. Choose any subject that might prove newsworthy (recycling efforts, new menu, announcement of softball team). Use the proper layout and design for your press release and include contact information, a heading, a good hook, and a succinct message. How will you follow up to ensure your press information will make it into the newspaper or trade journal?

Key Terms

- Report
- Document
- Memo
- Abstract
- Summary
- Business letter
- Identify the audience
- Organize the message
- Select the medium
- Write the draft
- Review and revise

- Draft
- Transition
- Salutation
- Closing
- Post Script
- Informational brochure
- Sales brochure
- Topic sentence
- Introduction
- Body
- Conclusion

- Recommendation
- Action plan
- Feasibility report
- Proposal
- Progress report
- Activity report
- Accident report
- Trip report
- Executive summary
- Abstract
- Press release

CHAPTER

3 | HUMAN RESOURCES

Tad Mitchell is the director of human resources for the Viviendo Resort & Conference Center, a medium-sized hospitality organization located in the Pacific northwest of the United States. He is responsible for overseeing recruitment, selection, training and development, performance reviews, compensation, and safety. Tad is responsible for a number of departments. It is his responsibility to oversee managers who, in turn, manage directly the supervisors for each department. Ultimately, Tad is responsible for making sure that rules, regulations, policies, and procedures are properly conducted throughout the operation.

Tad finds complaints, questions, comments, and concerns in his in-box on any given day. He knows that the communications produced by the department of human resources must be direct, clear, and concise. His communication, in one word, must be streamlined.

Ask any human relations professional and, like Tad Mitchell, he or she will tell you that the department of human relations is by far the most writing-intense department in industry. Fortunately, electronic communication has provided a means to ease up on the use of paper. Still, even with technology among the top "change items" for human resources, people still use hard copy for documentation, filing, and privacy.

In our litigious society, much of the documentation for each employee falls upon the shoulders of human resources. In my opinion, we do not give this department enough credit for the commitment to keeping things straight . . . just in case. It is also (frequently) this department's job to provide employees with various awards, training and development requirements, record-keeping, and a host of other details requiring forms, letters, announcements, and follow-through.

Introduction

This chapter discusses the various writing assignments given to human resource professionals, from preemployment to written verification of employment years after the employee leaves the company . . . and everything in between.

It should be noted that an employee leaving the company may be, in fact, employed in human resources. Written documentation stands the test of time, and employees should expect that they will get the same information about their job whoever is providing that very information.

For example, imagine that you are sued for discrimination a year after an employee left your company. Then, imagine that the human resource director is also no longer employed by your company. Do you want accurate records? Or, are you willing to risk that there are no written records to support your defense?

On the other hand, imagine you once worked for a company, consistently received accolades, and won the employee-of-the-year award. When your future employer wants to verify these claims, do you want them documented by your previous employer?

The human resources department clearly is involved in many types of writing. We discuss several of them next.

PREEMPLOYMENT

The aim of human resources is to become a preferred employer. The goal is to minimize the work of the department by hiring applicants who "FIT" the job. In human resource lingo: The aim of recruitment is to attract *qualified* job candidates.

Advertisements

Advertising job openings is changing. One means to recruit employees is newspaper advertisements. This form of advertisement reaches local people and might be the best way to recruit line workers. Students, a large constituency of the hospitality industry, are often local people looking for local jobs. Newspaper advertising is appropriate for part-time employment, seasonal employment, and temporary employment... especially for line-level jobs. Also, many local people read the "Want Ads," and so advertising pairs with marketing with regard to image and awareness.

Prepare a concise recruiting advertisement. If you look at your local newspaper, you will notice that certain ads jump out at you. What is it that makes these ads more appealing? Is it the placement? Is it the amount of negative or "white" space? Is the logo clear? Is the verbiage friendly and open?

Depending on how much you expect potential job applicants to screen themselves, your ad should be open. Consider the following when preparing an advertisement.

Be Positive

Recruit those who might fit your schedule in the text of the ad. For example, instead of saying

Must work weekends and evenings

You might say

Weekends and evening shifts available

Do you see the difference? The first example is negative and shuts people out. The second statement is positive and opens up the opportunity for people to see whether they are available for these shifts.

Include "White Space"

Layout is important. White space, or negative space, is space that you pay for but that you leave blank. You might begin and end your advertisement with white space. Although this will definitely cost more, it makes your advertisement stand out from the previous and following advertisements. It is often said that money spent on white space rather than text is money better spent.

For similar reasons, break your advertisement into paragraphs. Use bold type. Center important information. See the sample included here of an advertisement that makes good use of negative or white space.

Applications

Applications serve many purposes:

1. They are a great source of factual information.
2. They serve as documentation for Equal Employment Opportunity.
3. Questions are job-related.
4. Signatures are required.

Application forms can be purchased from any number of sources. Use them for line-level employees, when appropriate. If you do not have a formal employment procedure, the application form is a good substitute.

Internal Job Postings

Employee bulletin boards (electronic as well as those posted in the hallways next to the time clock) are the perfect way to post job announcements. There are several things in their favor, but there are also aspects of internal job postings that work against the employer.

Positives

- They are an inexpensive form of advertising.
- They get a quick response.
- They offer employees an opportunity for advancement.
- They provide employees with up-to-date employment information.
- Employees enjoy hearing about openings—they show you care.

At the same time, there are disadvantages to advertising "in-house":

Negatives

- They may result in "inbreeding."
- They may result in "group-think."
- There is a lower potential for creativity.
- There may be political overtones.

College Recruitment

Recruiting often requires outreach, including to colleges. Many large- to mid-sized companies have college relations programs that cater to recruiting both interns and recent graduates.

Sodexho

www.sodexhoUSA.com

SODEXHO EMPLOYMENT APPLICATION

APPLICATION FOR EMPLOYMENT

Name _____
      Last   First   Middle

Present Address _____

City _____ State _____ Zip _____ Telephone# _____

E-Mail Address _____ Alternative Telephone# _____

EMPLOYMENT INTEREST

Date _____ Position Applied for_____ Earliest Date Available_____

Salary Desired_____ Location Desired_____

Type of Employment Desired: ☐ Management ☐ Non-Management

                                      ☐ Full-time   ☐ Part-time   ☐ Temporary   ☐ On-call   ☐ Summer

How were you referred to Sodexho?   ☐ Ad   ☐ Web   ☐ Agency ☐ School   ☐ Employee ☐ Other

Please specify source: _____

Have you ever applied for work with or been employed by Sodexho Inc., Sodexho Marriott Services, Marriott Management Services, Sodexho USA or Wood Dining Services?   ☐ Yes   ☐ No   If yes, when and where? _____

If previously employed, please answer the following:

  Supervisor's Name, Title, and Phone#: _____

  Reason for Leaving: _____

If applying for a management position, are you willing to relocate?   ☐ Yes   ☐ No

  If yes, please specify where: _____

PERSONAL

Social Security# _____

For reference checking purposes, list all name(s) you have used or gone by in the past, if any, other than that listed above:

_____

_____

Are you over 18 years of age? ☐ Yes   ☐ No   If no, give date of birth _____

Have you ever been convicted of any felonies within the past seven (7) years? ☐ Yes   ☐ No   (A conviction will not necessarily disqualify you from employment with Sodexho.)
(Applicants need not disclose information pertaining to sealed or expunged conviction records.)

  If yes, give date, nature and place of conviction(s):_____

Are there any restrictions on the hours or day you are able to work?   ☐ Yes   ☐ No

  If yes, please explain: _____

Foreign Languages: _____ ☐ Read   ☐ Write   ☐ Speak

                                       _____ ☐ Read   ☐ Write   ☐ Speak

011 (09/03)

EDUCATIONAL HISTORY

Type of School	Name and Address of School	Dates Attended From: Month/Year	To: Month/Year	Graduated	Type of Degree, Diploma or Certificate	Major/Minor/ Field of Study
High School				☐ Yes ☐ No		
College or University				☐ Yes ☐ No		
Other Education or Training				☐ Yes ☐ No		

Academic Achievements or Activities: Please list academic honors, scholarships, or fellowships, memberships in academic honorary societies; or participation in or offices held in extracurricular activities you consider significant.

List current professional licenses, registration, and professional organizations or affiliates, if any.
(You must include license / registration numbers in specific states / jurisdictions where you may be licensed or registered.)

EMPLOYMENT EXPERIENCE

Please list your job history for the past six years (or last four employers), whichever list covers a longer period of time. Start with your present status and note any periods in which you were not employed. Include U.S. Military Service, previous Sodexho Inc., Sodexho Marriott Services, Marriott Management Services, Sodexho USA or Wood Dining Services experience, summer/part-time jobs, and cooperative education assignments.
This information must be completed even if a resume is provided.

Company Name	Date Started	Date Left	Starting Position
			Last Position
Address	Full Time	Part Time	
			Describe Major Duties:
Phone#	Starting Salary $	Final Salary $	
Reason for leaving:			
Name of Supervisor, Title, and Phone Number:		Additional References and Phone Number(s):	

Company Name	Date Started	Date Left	Starting Position
			Last Position
Address	Full Time	Part Time	
			Describe Major Duties:
Phone#	Starting Salary $	Final Salary $	
Reason for leaving:			
Name of Supervisor, Title, and Phone Number:		Additional References and Phone Number(s):	

Company Name	Date Started	Date Left	Starting Position
			Last Position
Address	Full Time	Part Time	
			Describe Major Duties:
Phone#	Starting Salary $	Final Salary $	
Reason for leaving:			
Name of Supervisor, Title, and Phone Number:		Additional References and Phone Number(s):	

Company Name	Date Started	Date Left	Starting Position
			Last Position
Address	Full Time	Part Time	
			Describe Major Duties:
Phone#	Starting Salary $	Final Salary $	
Reason for leaving:			
Name of Supervisor, Title, and Phone Number:		Additional References and Phone Number(s):	

Do you have any objections to our contacting your present employer to verify the above?

☐ No, you may contact anytime.

☐ Do not contact now. You may contact at a later date. _____
(Please specify, e.g. after acceptance of offer or a specific date, if appropriate.)

Have you ever been dismissed or forced to resign from employment? ☐ Yes ☐ No

If yes, please explain: _____
_____

PROFESSIONAL OR PERSONAL REFERENCES

Name	Years Known	Occupation	Complete Address	Telephone

Are any of your professional references associated with your current employer?

If yes, do you have any objection to our contacting that individual whose name you gave?

☐ No, you may contact anytime.

☐ Do not contact now. You may contact at a later date. _____
(Please specify, e.g. after acceptance of offer or a specific date, if appropriate.)

OTHER RELEVANT INFORMATION

Please include any other information you think would be helpful to us in considering you for employment, such as additional work experience, activities, accomplishments, etc.

_____
_____

(SIGNATURE REQUIRED ON BACK)

40

PLEASE READ THE FOLLOWING AGREEMENT CAREFULLY AND SIGN WHERE APPROPRIATE

ADDENDUM TO SODEXHO APPLICATION FOR MARYLAND

I understand that under Maryland law, an employer may not require or demand, as a condition of employment, prospective employment, or continued employment, that an individual submit to or take a lie detector or similar test. An employer who violates this law is guilty of a misdemeanor and subject to a fine not exceeding $100.00.

I have read and understand the above statement.

Applicant Signature

Applicant Printed Name   Date

ADDENDUM TO SODEXHO APPLICATION FOR CALIFORNIA

Regarding questions on felony convictions in the Personal Section of the Application Form:

Please exclude misdemeanor convictions for marijuana-related offenses more than two years old; convictions that have been sealed, expunged, or legally eradicated; and misdemeanor convictions for which probation was successfully completed or otherwise discharged and the case was judicially dismissed.

The company will not deny employment to any applicant solely because the person has been convicted of a crime. Each case will be evaluated based on its own facts and merits.

I have read and understand the above statement.

Applicant Signature

Applicant Printed Name   Date

ADDENDUM TO SODEXHO APPLICATION FOR CONNECTICUT

An applicant for employment need not disclose the existence of any arrest, criminal charge or conviction, the records of which have been erased pursuant to section 46b-146, 54-76o or 54-142a. Criminal records subject to erasure pursuant to Conn. Gen. Stat. section 46b-146, 54-76o or 54- 142a pertain to a finding of delinquency or that a child was a member of a family with service needs, an adjudication as a youthful offender, a criminal charge that has been dismissed or nolled, a criminal charge for which the person has been found not guilty or a conviction for which the person received an absolute pardon. Applicants whose records have been so erased shall be deemed to have never been arrested within the meaning of the general statutes with respect to the proceedings so erased and may so swear under oath.

I have read and understand the above statement.

Applicant Signature

Applicant Printed Name   Date

ADDENDUM TO SODEXHO APPLICATION FOR MASSACHUSETTS

It is unlawful in Massachusetts to require or administer a lie detector test as a condition of employment or continued employment. An employer who violates this law shall be subject to criminal penalties and civil liability.

An applicant for employment with a sealed record on file with the commissioner of probation may answer 'no record' with respect to an inquiry herein relative to prior arrests, criminal court appearances or convictions. In addition, any applicant for employment may answer 'no record' with respect to any inquiry relative to prior arrests, court appearances and adjudications in all cases of delinquency or as a child in need of services which did not result in a complaint transferred to the superior court for criminal prosecution.

I have read and understand the above statement.

Applicant Signature

Applicant Printed Name   Date

EQUAL EMPLOYMENT OPPORTUNITY EMPLOYER

Sodexho does not discriminate in hiring or employment on the basis of race, color, religion, national origin, sex, age, disability, veteran status or on any other basis protected by law. If needed, reasonable accommodations for the hiring process will be made.

AUTHORIZATION AND RELEASE

The information that I have provided is accurate to the best of my knowledge and subject to validation by Sodexho. I understand and agree that any misrepresentation or omission of a fact in my application may be justification for not being hired or, if hired, termination of any employment with Sodexho.

I understand that an offer of employment and my continued employment with Sodexho are contingent upon satisfactory proof of my authorization to work in the United States. I understand that nothing contained in this employment application or in the granting of an interview is intended to create an employment contract between myself and Sodexho for either employment or for the providing of any benefit. No promises regarding continued employment have been made to me, and I understand that no such promise or guarantee is binding upon Sodexho unless made in writing. I understand that my employment is terminable at-will, and that either I or my employer may terminate my employment at any time, with or without, cause, for any or no reason, and that I am not being employed for any specific term.

I understand that business needs at times make conditions such as the following mandatory: overtime, shift work, and rotating work schedules. I understand and accept these conditions of my employment.

I understand that under Sodexho policy and applicable law, applicants will not be asked to take a lie detector or polygraph test.

I authorize a thorough investigation of my educational background, past employment and activities that may relate in any way to my potential fitness for employment with Sodexho.

I authorize schools and prior employers to provide any information they have concerning me to Sodexho, and I hereby hold harmless Sodexho and all those providing information from any liability that may arise out of or result from the provision or use of such information.

Applicant Signature

I understand that I may be required to take and pass a drug test as a condition of being hired at or transferred to a Sodexho location

I have read and understand the above statement.

Applicant Printed Name   Date

SOURCE: Sodexho USA.

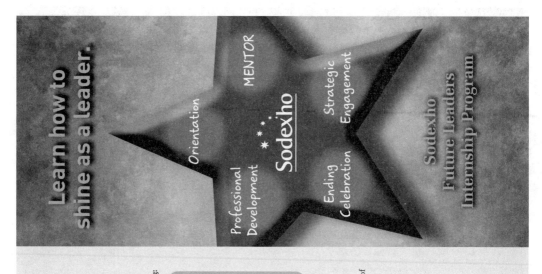

Learn how to
shine as a leader.

MENTOR

Orientation

Strategic
Engagement

Sodexho
★ ★
★ ★
★
Sodexho

Professional
Development

Ending
Celebration

Sodexho
Future Leaders
Internship Program

The Sodexho Future Leaders Internship Program offers an exciting opportunity for college students to turn their leadership potential into valuable professional experience and to get a head start on their careers.

The mission of the Sodexho Future Leaders Internship Program is to provide world-class professional development opportunities to college students that result in organization-wide position placements.

The Future Leaders Internship Program provides outstanding exposure to the contract management services industry. Interns are encouraged and expected to make an impact immediately. Interns will learn the power of diversity, peer support and excellent client service.

For consideration, please submit the following:

1. Your current resume

2. A 250-word essay that addresses the following questions:
   - What type of internship are you seeking?
   - Why are you seeking an internship with Sodexho?
   - What do you hope to gain from the internship?

3. Letter of recommendation from a faculty member

E-mail your resume, essay and letter of recommendation to internships@sodexhousa.com.

Learn more about Sodexho and our full range of internship and career opportunities at:

www.sodexhoUSA.com

Successful completion of an internship will not be a guarantee of full-time employment with Sodexho. EOE. M/F/D/V

Unique Features

To enhance your experience both during and after an internship, this unique program includes five major components.

Managers Engaging Nurturing & Training Our Recruits (MENTOR) Program: You'll be paired with one of our middle or senior-level managers, representing a variety of culturally diverse backgrounds and career interests. This relationship will continue through the duration of your college career and beyond.

Orientation: Your experience begins with a program kickoff that will introduce you to Sodexho and give you the opportunity to connect with your MENTOR, corporate staff, and other interns.

Professional Development: Learning resources include one-hour webinars covering such topics as employee networks, getting the most out of your MENTOR relationship, negotiating a job offer, post-college career strategies and more.

Ending Celebration: At the program's completion, you'll celebrate lessons learned and set the stage for future strategic engagement with Sodexho.

Strategic Engagement: As a former intern, you may be: invited to serve on the Future Leaders Internship Program Planning Committee; asked to represent the company on campus as a Sodexho Ambassador; or featured in the campus relations e-newsletter.

Choose Your Internship

At Sodexho, you can choose to apply your talent and ambition toward becoming a leader in a variety of settings.

Whichever you choose, you'll learn how to lead and motivate your team to provide exceptional service to guests, clients, patients, or even the U.S. Marine Corps! You'll also experience firsthand the importance of fostering the development of all team members through mentoring, and you'll see the benefits of our unmatched nationwide network of support.

Areas of internship opportunity include:

Food Service Management

Environmental Services/ Housekeeping Management

Facilities – Maintenance/ Engineering Management

> *Interested in a marketing, human resources, communications, accounting or other internship opportunity? Please ask for availability.*

Details & Qualifications

Program Details:
- 10-week duration, with 40-hour weeks
- Earn $460 per week
- Locations in select facilities (we will attempt to place interns in proximity to home or school)

Qualifications:
- Major in hospitality/food management, facilities management, mechanical/electrical engineering, communications, human resources, accounting, marketing or other industry-related program
- Be a rising sophomore, junior or graduate student
- Preference will be given to those with a strong record of community service and leadership

SOURCE: Sodexho USA.

43

College graduates often have many companies to select from based on their college's recruiting program. It comes down to distinguishing between "the great companies to work for" and "those companies where I'll take a job."

SELECTION

Selection is the next step in recruiting and is distinguished from it by the type of writing involved in the process. The selection process includes a checklist of traits to be observed during the interview.

THE FISHING ANALOGY

Seeking employees is like fishing.

Recruiting is throwing out the fishing pole—you want to cast far and wide, but in areas where you know the fish are hiding.

Selection is reeling back the fish you attract—you want the best, the most qualified, for your company. Then you want to be able to make a decision about which to throw back and which to keep.

Many people may be involved in the process of hiring, including human resources, department heads, supervisors, and other employees. It is important to organize for each person the forms and checklists that will be included in the final decision to hire or to not to hire. This does not have to be a cumbersome task, but it does need to be streamlined.

A selection checklist should include the following:

- Technical skills
- Previous experience
- Strengths and weaknesses
- Special interests
- References

In addition, hospitality requires special interpersonal skills that should be considered in the selection process:

- Eye contact
- Knowledge
- Respect for the job
- Smile
- Interpersonal skills
- Team player
- Hygiene
- Flexible schedule

- Work at home
- Transportation available
- Child care available
- Happiness factor
- Legal requirements

"Interview Check List"

Name:
Pre Interview

Job Description:	1	2	3	4	5	6	7
Cover letter:	1	2	3	4	5	6	7

Resume: 1 2 3 4 5 6 7
- Written
- Style
- Consistent
- Depth of knowledge for the job

Reference List: 1 2 3 4 5 6 7
Complete info
Three references

At the Interview
Verbal Skills: 1 2 3 4 5 6 7
- Vocal: Pronunciation; Inflections; Tone; Pace; Volume
- Articulation: No filler phrases; Specificity

Non-Verbal Skills: 1 2 3 4 5 6 7
- On time
- Appearance
- Posture & movement
- Gestures: Natural; No nervous habits
- Eye Contact

Interpersonal Skills: 1 2 3 4 5 6 7
- Smile
- Handshake
- Poise
- Rapport
- Sense of humor

Areas of strength:

Areas for improvement:

Additional Comments:

REJECTION LETTERS

Some companies choose to send rejection letters to applicants not chosen for the job. Rejection letters are usually expected if the short list is three or fewer people. They bring closure to the process. Some companies never send rejection letters, deciding to focus only on applicants they wish to hire, and never explain to others that a final decision has been made.

An appropriate rejection letter is shown next. Note that the letter is noncommittal and generally positive and serves to bring closure to the employment process. It is not advisable to invite unsuccessful applicants to contact the company about reasons they were not selected. That being said, many applicants want to know what the successful applicant had that he or she did not have. For these cases, human resources should have a procedure in place.

Date

Dear Mr./Ms. Name:

We congratulate you on your qualifications for the position of Food and Beverage Director for the XYZ Company. As you know, several qualified applicants were considered for the position, and we have made our decision.

After careful consideration and reviews, we have selected another candidate who has accepted the position as Food and Beverage Director at XYZ. We believe your credentials to be very good, but we also regret to inform you that you were not selected for this position.

Please know that we are most grateful that you considered employment with our company. We wish you the very best in your future endeavors.

Respectfully,

Amanda S. Smith
Director
Human Resources

JOB DESCRIPTIONS

Job descriptions are statements of a job's essential duties, responsibilities, working conditions, and specifications. Job descriptions provide information about the Knowledge, Skills, and Abilities (KSAs) required for any job.

JOB TITLE: Kitchen Manager

POSITION PURPOSE:

The purpose of this position is to maintain a safe and efficient kitchen through directing and supervising activities of personnel and providing management support for the executive chef.

JOB DUTIES:

1. Direct activities of all kitchen personnel during a specific shift.
2. Issue written communication to kitchen personnel, particularly policies and operational concerns that affect the entire operation and mission statement for the company.
3. Administer cleaning and maintenance program through requests, scheduling and recording of cleaning, and maintenance activities.
4. Conduct training and safety programs for personnel under direct supervision.
5. Schedule assignments to reflect individual workload and vacation schedules.
6. Perform administrative tasks such as maintaining time records, maintenance records, and written procedures.
7. Maintain inventory of kitchen equipment and supplies.
8. Assist in performance appraisal of employees under direct supervision.
9. Counsel employees on disciplinary problems and job-related performance.
10. Delegate tasks as deemed necessary.

PHYSICAL REQUIREMENTS:

Walking. Must lift at least fifty (50) pounds. Ability to stand for eight hours per day.

WORKING CONDITIONS:

Good, must be able to work in heated environment.

EQUIPMENT & MACHINES USES:

All kitchen equipment to include cooking, dishwashing, and other equipment. Utilities to include knife skills.

REPORTING RELATIONSHIPS:

The kitchen manager reports directly to the executive chef. The kitchen manager directs the operations of the kitchen, five or more cooks, trainees, one or more dishwashers, and other assigned personnel. The kitchen manager must interact effectively with other managers and personnel in the food and beverage department, such as banquet manager, dining room manager, servers, and food runners.

QUALIFICATIONS:

Education: Associate degree or equivalent training (e.g., management training classes) OR three (3) years of management experience.

Other Related Experience: Minimum of three (3) years as a cook.

JOB KNOWLEDGE/SKILLS REQUIRED:

1. Full understanding of kitchen equipment.
2. Thorough knowledge of cooking to include ability to write and follow recipes.
3. Performance of elementary mathematical and algebraic calculations.
4. Communication and human relations skills to include written and oral communication.
5. Ability to operate computer.
6. Ability to operate telephone; leave articulate and clear messages.
7. Basic to advanced managerial skills.
8. Sense of urgency.
9. Ability to get along well with others.

Job descriptions are crucial to set standards, to provide criteria for performance evaluations, to determine pay structure, and to validate selection procedures. Furthermore, job descriptions identify training needs and objectives. In short, job descriptions help to decide the type of worker needed to succeed in a job.

Components of a job description include:

Job Identification Data

- Title
- Work area
- Supervisor's name
- Pay range

Job Summary

- Brief, general statement that highlights common responsibilities

Job Duties

- Tasks
- Responsibilities

Note: These require action verbs.

Job Specifications

- A list of minimum qualifications for the job: Knowledge, Skills, Abilities

Action Verbs

Using specific, precise, descriptive verbs to describe each job duty (such as "organize" or "budget" rather than general verbs such as "manage" or "oversee") helps to define jobs. These same action verbs can be used both for writing a job description or your own resume. Action verbs help to quantify and measure the tasks (or KSAs) for success.

ORIENTATION

Once an employee is hired, the orientation process begins. It is best to maintain an orientation checklist for the employee file. Each item on the orientation checklist should include the initials of both the person providing the orientation and the employee. It always should include the date.

ACTION VERBS

CLERICAL SKILLS

Arrange
Catalogue
Compile
Generate
Organize
Process
Systematize

CREATIVE SKILLS

Conceptualize
Create
Design
Establish
Fashion
Illustrate
Invent
Perform

COMMUNICATION SKILLS

Arrange
Address
Author
Draft
Formulate
Persuade

FINANCIAL SKILLS

Administer
Analyze
Balance
Budget
Forecast
Market
Plan
Project

HELPING SKILLS

Assess
Coach
Counsel
Diagnose
Facilitate
Represent

MANAGEMENT SKILLS

Administer
Analyze
Coordinate
Develop
Direct
Evaluate
Improve
Supervise

RESEARCH SKILLS

Clarify
Evaluate
Identify
Inspect
Organize
Summarize

TECHNICAL SKILLS

Assemble
Build
Calculate
Design
Operate
Overhaul
Remodel
Repair

Orientation Checklist

The following orientation was conducted for

_____ **Name of employee**

By

_____   **Name of trainer**

_____   _____

Date and signed   **Date and signed**

Tour of the facility to include:

_____ History

Employment policies (manual)

_____ Received

Preview

Work hours

Salary/Check delivery

Benefits

_____Insurance & related benefits

_____Hospitalization

_____Profit sharing/Incentive plan

_____Educational assistance plan

_____Cultural exchange program

_____House rules

_____Time off

_____Vacation

_____Scheduling procedure

_____Holidays

_____Sick days

_____Bereavement leave

_____Jury duty

_____Medial leaves of absence

_____Military leave

House Rules

_____Gum chewing

_____Smoking

_____Drug-free workplace

_____Use of telephone

_____Use of email

_____Use of personal mail

_____Parking

_____Check cashing/payroll advances

_____Food on premises

Arrival & Departure

_____Entrance

_____Guest

_____employee

_____Exit

_____Guest

_____Employee

Location of:

_____Personnel office

_____Schedule

_____Time clock

_____Rooms

_____Front desk

_____Restaurant

_____Laundry

_____Employee lounge

_____Introductions to all personnel

_____Expectations of etiquette and attitude

_____Voluntary separations

_____Overview of the training manual

_____Overview of the next two weeks of training – to occur on:

_____

Date

EMPLOYEE REVIEWS (OR PREVIEWS)

Human resource professionals are frequently required to update employee files regarding performance evaluations. These evaluations can be conducted in many ways; however, it is advisable to maintain a systematic review policy.

For example, you might opt to review employees after 90 days of employment and on their annual anniversary date. This is a recommended policy, but it is entirely up to the company to decide when to review employees. Incidentally, a raise is not always considered automatic with employment reviews.

Employee reviews are helpful in identifying strengths and weaknesses and measuring, and managing all employees. Frequently, reviews are conducted by individual department heads or supervisors. Nonetheless, it is the responsibility of the human resources department to ensure that all employee reviews meet the standards of federal and state laws and are performed consistently.

Some companies refer to employee reviews as "employee previews." I like this attitude! It shows a positive, forward-looking response to evaluating employees. It also dispels the idea that everything is a review of the past—it's so much more rewarding to look toward the future! Also, the idea of presenting employee performance evaluations as a "preview" rather than a "review" does away with the top-down approach. It supports the idea that employees are internal customers we wish to keep with the company.

The main idea with employee performance evaluations is to be forward thinking (i.e., *preview*) and not retrospective (i.e., *review*). Clearly, the review is part of the evaluation, but putting the past in the context of the future helps employees and managers feel better about the process. It offers opportunity for feedback and identifies ways to improve. All these are potential cost-saving policies for any hospitality company.

This is a preview form given to employees at least one week before the scheduled preview.

PREVIEW FORM

A preview is scheduled for you at your 90-day and annual anniversary date. The purpose is to discuss openly the direction or course you intend to follow in your future employment with the company and also to work along the lines of career goals. Please take time to carefully answer the following questions and bring this completed form with you to the preview.

1. Looking toward the future, in what way do you wish to develop your performance, and how can your supervisor help you to achieve those improvements?
2. What long-term goals for personal development or achievement do you have? How can your supervisor help you to achieve them?
3. What long-term objectives for personal and professional development do you have? How can your supervisor help you to achieve them?
4. How well do you think you have performed since your last interview? Give specific examples, details, information, etc.
5. Any additional comments?

Preview Form (completed at the time of the preview)

Name   Date
Department   Position
Supervisor   Preview: 90 day
                                                         Annual

General Performance:

Punctual: Yes _____   No _____

Grooming: Very Good   _____
                 Satisfactory   _____
                 Needs improvement   _____

Foundation Skills:

Excellent: _____   Very Good _____   Good _____   Satisfactory _____   Poor _____

Constructive Comments:

Areas of Distinction:

Areas to be developed:

Comments/Questions:

Goals for the next Month

Goals for the Next Year:

Signature: _____   _____
                  Employee   Supervisor

                  _____   _____
                  Manager   Date

EMPLOYEE EXIT INTERVIEW

Probably the most pain-in-the-neck interview that human resource professionals perform is the exit interview. Think about it: This person is leaving your employ; this person
no longer represents your company; this person is past and you are working on the present and the future. So, why conduct an employee exit interview?

Well, the answer is simple—you learn a lot. Employees leaving your establishment
may be leaving on good or bad terms. It doesn't matter. You can get good feedback
from them. Usually for employees leaving the company, there is no risk in disclosure.
You may or may not get workable feedback, but you will always get something worth
considering.

Employee exit interviews take little time and should be conducted in a nonthreat-
ening manner by a person from human resources. Supervisors, however, should always
be included in reviewing the results. Perhaps the interview could be done by mail.

Animosity is a plus, and managers learn a great deal by providing it. A stamped, self-addressed envelope should be handed out at any employee exit interview.

Do not consider the employee exit interview as a direct attack on you or your company. The more you do not take personally the reasons for an employee's leaving, the better off you will be.

Employee Exit Interview

Name _____ Today's date _____

     Optional

Position _____ Department _____

Hire date _____ Leave date _____

Please rate the following:

	Excellent	Very Good	Good	Fair	Poor	Comments
Your supervisor						
Your co-workers						
Your job						
Your schedule						
Working conditions						
Wages						
Opportunity for advancement						
Communication						

What did you like best about your job:

_____

_____

_____

What did you dislike about your job:

_____

_____

_____

Would you have preferred another job or department in our organization, and if so, what and why?

_____

_____

_____

Reason for terminating:

_____

_____

_____

Would you recommend other to seek employment with our company? _____ yes _____ no
Comments:

_____

_____

_____

LETTER OF RECOMMENDATION AND VERIFICATION OF EMPLOYMENT

Some companies have strict rules about writing letters of recommendation using company letterhead. Usually, managers are trusted to write a letter of recommendation for an employee, and it is assumed that the letter is particular to that manager. Other times, perhaps as an employee leaves the company, a verification of employment is more applicable.

The difference is important in that the letter of recommendation serves as a reference to endorse employment for a previous employee. The letter of verification suffices to document that a person was employed between certain dates and is (or is not) eligible for rehire.

The distinction between the two is important. For example, a letter of verification might suffice for a bank loan application, while a letter of recommendation might apply to endorsing employment with another company.

Typically, the human resource department deals with the letter of verification. This document verifies three items, which were determined by the courts:

✓ Beginning date of employment
✓ Ending date of employment
✓ Eligibility for rehire: yes or no

These three items are important because they determine future records for employees, and they should be documented in the employee's file. They are nonjudgmental. The only area for subjective opinion here is "eligibility for rehire," which pertains to any legal reason that makes the ex-employee eligible or not. This should be documented in all employees' files.

The verification of employment form should not be thought of as rude. Some companies simply have a direct approach to dealing with past employees, given previous experiences. Those supplying and checking employment references should be aware of these policies.

"Verification of Employment Form"

_____
Name of employee

Was employed by the above company from _____ to
_____.

According to our employee files, the above named employee CIRCLE ONE:

is

is not

eligible for rehire.

Thank you for your enquire,

Amanda S. Smith
Director
Human Resources

Letter of Recommendation

Letters of recommendation are above and beyond verification of employment. Anyone can obtain a letter of verification, which states the facts. You should know a few things about letters of recommendation:

> You do not owe any employee a letter of recommendation.
> There are levels of endorsement in letters of recommendation.
> A letter of recommendation should be sincere—your name is attached!

In my many reviews of letters of recommendation I have observed "subtle" messages, including:

- You should seriously think about hiring this employee (verification only).
- I feel compelled to write this letter, but I don't really mean it because I'm eager to get rid of this employee.
- It is difficult to write this letter because I really don't want this employee to leave.
- The best advancement opportunity for this employee is to leave this company and explore other opportunities.

When employees leave, a company may feel one of three ways: (1) we provide verification only; (2) we are indifferent and wish them our best; or (3) we really don't want them to leave, but we will support their efforts to succeed. The tone of references is obvious to those receiving these letters. Observe the three examples presented here and compare.

We are providing verification of employment.

Dear Future Employer:

Charlie Castanos was employed by the XYZ Company from September 1, 2005 to December 31, 2005.

Mr. Castonos was employed as a Maintenance Operator in our Maintenance Department. He performed the duties required of the department on a regular basis and achieved a passing grade on his performance reviews.

Further requests for information can be obtained from our Human Resources Department.

Sincerely,

Amanda W. Biddle, Director
Human Resources
XYZ Company

We provide verification and slight recommendation—we are indifferent and wish them our best.

Dear Future Employer:

Charlie Castanos was employed by the XYZ Company from September 1, 2005 to December 31, 2005.

Mr. Castonos was employed as a Maintenance Operator in our Maintenance Department. He performed the duties required of the department on a regular basis and achieved an exemplary grades on his performance reviews.

Mr. Castonos was always willing to help guests and other employees when the opportunity was available. For example, when Mr. Castonos was about to end his duties for the day and an emergency occurred, he was available to extend his hours to ensure the problems were taken care of.

I can recall one time, in particular, when a front desk clerk checked a guest into a room that had not been cleared by maintenance. The HVAC was not working in that room for some reason. Mr. Castonos was working in the hallway at the time and, noticing the valet checking the guest into that room, alerted the front desk that the room was not ready for occupancy. For some reason, the communications between Housekeeping and Front Desk was not up-to-the moment (our usual policy). He alerted the Front Desk and the guest was reasonably reaccommodated.

Thanks to efforts like those of Mr. Castonos, we were able to maintain our standards. I commend him for his efforts to speak out on behalf of the team. Not all employees react like this, and I commend Mr. Castonos for his efforts.

Please let me know if I can be of further assistance.

Sincerely,

Eric V. Smith, Director
Food and Beverage Department
XYZ Company

Amanda W. Biddle, Director
Human Resources
XYZ Company

We really like this employee and don't want him/her to leave, but we will support his/her efforts to succeed.

May 5, 20xx

Letter of Support for Daniel Klein for Employment

Please accept this letter as a reference and recommendation for Daniel Klein for a position with your company. I have known Daniel Klein for two years now, since he took my undergraduate communications course during his junior year. Daniel was also a student in my human resource management course during his senior year. In my long teaching career, I rarely meet undergraduate students with such a genuine and focused interest in hospitality—and such a clear aptitude for it. Daniel is a superb candidate for any position related to hospitality and I will demonstrate this by speaking to his ability as a communicator, his specific interest in food and beverage, and his maturity and integrity.

Even during his junior year, Daniel was a skilled communicator on the subject of hospitality. Daniel worked diligently on his business writing, his speaking skills, and his interpersonal communication while he was student in my class. Although he was a clear leader, he was always open to learning more. He works well in group activities and individually. He articulates his message well and is both admired and well liked by his peers. For me, such abilities underscore what is so important in the hospitality industry: to get along well with others, to be creative, to understand and respect one's place, and to take care of other's needs with empathy and finesse.

Frequently, I witnessed Daniel's interactions with his peers and professors and know first-hand of his work with the Penn State Hotel and Restaurant Society. Daniel was instrumental in recruiting other students to join the club. He also worked to make the trip to the New York Hotel Show a success. He interacts with both the students and the faculty in a mature fashion. I have seen him handle delicate situations with discretion and poise.

Finally, Daniel is a person of strong character. He maintains good judgment; he is close with his family; he embraces diversity. It is a rare treat to encounter a student as impressive as Daniel Klein; and if you give him the opportunity, I am sure you will find him equally impressive.

Sincerely,

Vivienne J. Wildes, Ph.D.
Assistant Professor

Chapter Questions and Exercises

1. Name four types of writing used during the preemployment process.
2. What is the difference between a review and a preview?
3. How does professional appearance affect an applicant's recruitment process?
4. Design an advertisement for a key position in your company.
5. Define and distinguish between the following terms:
   - verification of employment
   - recommendation for a job
6. Write a letter of recommendation for yourself. What are your accomplishments? Do you have any areas of concern? Provide specific examples of ways in which you succeed in your job.
7. Obtain and analyze job descriptions for you own job and for those who work both above and under you. Is the job description accurate? What do you think can be added to the job description?

Key Terms

- Preemployment
- Advertisement
- Application
- Internal job posting
- College recruitment
- Interview check list
- Rejection letter
- Job description
- Action verbs
- Orientation checklist
- Preview form
- Exit interview
- Verification of employment
- Recommendation

4

SALES AND CATERING

Brian Morrell has decided after years of working in hotel catering to start his own company. Years of assisting his bosses have left him with the impression that he has the skills to do it himself. As a former hotel chef, preparing hundreds of dishes for customers day after day and night after night, his culinary skills are there. A location has been rented not too far from his home, which will make the commute easier, and already some of his former workers have agreed to moonlight and help him get his business going while they earn some extra cash. He talked it over with his boss and they agreed that his business would go after different accounts, so there was not a problem if he still wanted to keep his current job at the hotel part-time. Everything seemed to be falling into place until one day he sat down at his computer to write to a person whom he had heard through the grapevine really enjoyed his cooking and wanted to hire his new company for a private party at the client's house. He had never played in the world of catering writing and sat there looking at his computer....

Introduction

The goal of this chapter is to complement the current and future manager's skill set with catering writing capabilities. Being good, like Brian, is not enough when information needs to be conveyed professionally. Let's add writing to his career toolkit.

From off-site weddings to trade shows to special events, catering covers a wide array of venues. Most professionals will confess that rarely are any two events alike. The amount of planning that goes into an event that spans a comparatively short amount of time can be staggering. Trained catering professionals, like all others in hospitality, know the importance of presentation. The goal is a tight ship that the client does not notice, rather the smooth sailing.

Like most other business writing in hospitality, writing done in the catering department is one of the few "tangible" outcomes of an event. The rest are photos and memories with perhaps a parting gift. The event, however much planning has gone into it, comes and goes. The writing itself lasts to serve both as a written record of the event and possibly as an aid for the client and manager to be used for future events. It is therefore important that much effort be put into any catering writing. Here are the six primary areas of catering writing:

Writing Flow in Catering

1. Understanding your business and target markets →
2. Forecasting→
3. The marketing letter→
4. The proposal→
5. Invoice/follow-up letter→
6. Internal follow-up and revisions

To the catering professional, steps 2–4 seem logical and will be described in detail shortly. Steps 1 and 6, while no more important than the others, are ones that speak to businesses longevity. Let's start at the beginning.

UNDERSTANDING YOUR BUSINESS AND TARGET MARKETS

What is your business's sweet spot? Weddings? Corporate lunches? Sporting events? Is yours just a seasonal business? Are you part of a hotel or convention center or are you an off-site kitchen? How big can you go? These and many other questions must be answered before any writing can begin. It may seem, particularly to new businesses, that they take what they can get. However, taking on an account that may be too large or too specialized can result in a bad event that is witnessed by many who could quickly spread the negative word, and we all know how quickly bad news or reviews travel. No matter how long you have been in business or how large you are, let's run through a "make sure you know your capabilities" checklist.

What type of catering business are you (barbeque versus fine dining)?
What is your price structure?
What is the maximum amount of guests you can handle?
What is the minimum?
What does your business do really well?
What does it do poorly?
What is your maximum travel distance?
Is yours a seasonal or year-round business?
What places do you not do?
What is the maximum amount of courses/beverages you can provide?
Does your insurance cover all applicable events?
Are there any local ordinances that need to be observed?
What is your ratio of staff to guests?
What is the maximum amount of staff you can comfortably manage?
What are your partners' strengths and weaknesses?
What is your deposit minimum?
Are you responsible for your guests' automobiles?
Do you provide entertainment?
Are you better at off-site or on-site? (e.g., hotel)

What technology will you use?
Who is your competition?
What do they do well?
What don't they do well?
Who are their clients?

This last question raises a critical point regarding your competitors' customers. Understanding as best you can just how many clients they have (i.e., accounts) can give you a handle on just how big your market is. It also provides you with an immediate list of potential customers, who may be in want of a change or had no idea there was another option in their area. Your competition can also serve as a great source for evaluating writing samples. Just as you are sure that your crab dip tastes a whole lot better than your competitors', because people have told you so, the same applies to written presentations. Get some feedback from a good cross section of individuals on your competitors' literature. Larger companies will often outsource this function to a consulting or advertising firm specializing in marketing literature or print advertising. This may be unreasonable for your business, but you can at least do a nonscientific poll of as many people as you think wise (at least over 10) of basic questions about their likes, dislikes, and recommended changes to the literature.

Armed with information about your own businesses capabilities, a further understanding of your target market, and insight into your competitors' clients and literature (we'll leave the food and service to other textbooks), you can move on to forecasting.

FORECASTING

With a specific understanding of clients and how you can serve them, many times what you need is financing. New and existing businesses often need working capital that exceeds their current means. At this point, they turn to family and friends, interested investors, or a bank. This section covers the writing necessary to securing a loan or other types of underwriting.

Although no investors are alike, they all may require certain answers to the same questions. Let's take a look at the categories that need to be covered. The following is also known as a business plan.

Business Description: Here you detail the type of outfit you are operating, such as "A local fine-dining catering serving the corporate and retail sector."

Company Background: Names of founders and dates of incorporation and the like: "ABC catering was founded in 2005 by Paul Howard in State College Pennsylvania meeting a true market need."

Management and Staff: Detailed description of the management and staff expertise and experience: "With our award-winning chef and an experienced fine-dining staff. . . ."

Product/Services: Adding to the details in the business description, this section describes exactly what you offer: "At our on-site or off-site events, our staff and equipment consist of the following in meeting our client's needs. . . ."

Special Know-How: What you do better and differently belongs here: "With our dedication to French and Italian cuisine, paired with the finest and extensive wine offerings, our knowledgeable staff. . . ."

Markets: Your knowledge based on your research described earlier in the chapter is spelled out here, where the potential investor is shown that you have done your homework on the market potential and what piece of it you may be able to obtain: "Given the current population growth in our immediate area and rising school enrollments of X% and current competitive analysis, we estimate the market in our immediate area to be. . . ."

Vendor Relations: What you purchase and serve your clients is of the highest importance. Having specific contacts and possibly exclusives for certain products are detailed here: "With our experienced purchasers and our exclusive agreement with XYZ wine imports, we are the only company in the immediate metropolitan area able to offer such fine products. . . ."

Competition: In light of the introduction to this chapter, a no-holds-barred description is needed here. If you underestimate your competitors, or don't present them as a threat, you may lose your investors. Knowing your competition is the key. Let investors know you understand the playing field: "While JKL catering is currently the market leader in corporate and retail catering in our immediate area, our belief is that the market is ready for something new. . . ."

Financials: Detailed financials are inserted here, with projected revenues and detailed expenses for at least a three-year period.

The length of the business plan varies; a minimum of ten pages, in addition to in-depth financial statements, is a good rule of thumb and shows investors that you are serious.

THE MARKETING LETTER

Understanding what goes into a "good" marketing letter is the first step in creating one. What should be included may seem obvious, but we need to emphasize it here. What holds true for movie print advertisements that include reviewers' comments like "Best Comedy of the Summer" is also true for catering promotional material. A great quote about your company from a well-known client in your market is ideal—someone speaking on your behalf is important. Given that this content is included in all marketing materials, we will discuss the two main types of marketing letters, solicited and unsolicited.

Solicited Letters

Solicited letters are sent in response to a request by a potential customer, whether, for example, over the phone, in person, or by e-mail. This is the literature that you send out in answer to the question: "Can you send me some information about your company?" Often, catering companies will hear secondhand of someone who is looking for a caterer, which we consider a solicited inquiry. Whatever the case, the solicited marketing letter is focused and tailored to a specific request.

Much of the same logic used in the last section applies here. Although at this point you do not know what the client specifically wants, when you know who they are, you are better able to discern their needs. Whatever literature you have, therefore, should be fine-tuned to this customer. Say the request comes from a corporate client; leave out the wedding expertise (for now) and stress your corporate themes and offerings. Most catering companies stick with a one-size-fits-all approach in their marketing material, which can be mistake. It is important to show your potential client that you are a specialist in what they desire.

Keeping in mind that we are still in the marketing letter stage and not quite into the proposal stage, lets list the specifics of what the letter should contain:

1. Professional company overhead with a few pictures if possible
2. An introduction
3. Points of expertise that match the request (remember keep it targeted)
4. Referrals!
5. Your name and contact information

Professional Company Letterhead

Letterhead varies from company to company. What is important is that it contain the necessary contact information, presented in a professional manner. Pictures are included when necessary to represent a specific type of event—wedding pictures for weddings and corporate shots for business affairs.

Introduction

The opening deserves a lot of attention. The beginning of the letter needs to capture your potential client immediately. Since this is a solicited letter, it can be personalized. How much do you know about your potential client? How much do they know about you? Did they attend a past event that they enjoyed? Again, this letter is personalized to give you a leg up on any other marketing letters the client may be receiving. An example of an introduction in a solicited letter follows:

> Dear Mrs. Krall:
>
> Thank you very much for considering ABC catering for your daughter's upcoming wedding. We hope you enjoyed your neighbor's event, where we showcased some, but by no means all, of our specialties for these special times in life. From fresh, reasonably priced seafood to traditional cuisine, our experienced staff is here to meet your every need.

What has this introduction accomplished? First, it established a connection with the client through a referral. Second, it let the potential customer know that what she experienced at the past event is just one of many of your company's offerings—you have lots more! Third, it let the client know that hers is a very important occasion to the company. Remember, if someone is having an event catered, it is most likely a special occasion. Finally, the last sentence lets the client know that the company understands price and staffing concerns. Other aspects such as location, time of year, and others may be included, depending on what is known about the potential customer.

Points of Expertise That Match the Request

Again, with a solicited letter you have the advantage of knowing more about the client than you do with an unsolicited request. Now it is time to focus on exactly what the client needs and how your company can satisfy those needs. Specifically, satisfying the request can include the following:

1. Your level of service (black tie, casual, unseen, etc.)
2. Your experience with the location
3. Food choices that match the client's request
4. Presentation of food that matches the client's request (buffet, butlered, etc.)
5. Beverage choice and presentation (open bar, table service, etc.)
6. Parking, gift bags, etc.
7. Special extras that your company does best

Let's look at the next paragraph in the solicited letter:

> We at ABC catering offer a wide array of themes to meet your specific needs. From black tie to Hawaiian shirts or, if you wish, behind the scenes, your event is your event. Having expertise with and contacts for many of the various locations [insert locations here], our award-winning chef and staff will deliver beyond your expectations.

Have all the criteria been met? What else might you include? What else might you exclude?

Referrals

Here you include the praises of your happy current and past clients. Having the inside track of the potential client already knowing something positive about you, you can now use that to your advantage. It is important that you do not overdo here: You have already been referred and made the short list; overselling can be too much. The key here is to reference the high points of your past event that the potential client attended or aspects of the event that the client enjoyed.

> Next paragraph:

> As you have already seen and tasted, we at ABC offer wine and cheese pairings for the first course, served by a knowledgeable staff. In the past, the tastings and commentary have always pleased our guests, as have the literature and reference web sites made available to all guests and included in the gift bag, if desired. Just let us know your specific requirements and we will work with you to impress and make the evening a memorable event.

Your Name and Contact Information

Most company stationery contains the necessary contact information at the top of the letterhead as well as at the bottom in a smaller form. Let's look at our letter in its entirety.

Company Logo and Contact Information Here

Dear Mrs. Krall:

Thank you very for considering ABC catering for your daughter's upcoming wedding. We hope you enjoyed your neighbor's event, where we showcased some, but by no means all, of our specialties for these special times in life. From fresh, reasonably priced seafood to traditional cuisine, our experienced staff is here to meet your every need.

We at ABC catering offer a wide array of themes to meet your specific needs. From black tie to Hawaiian shirts or, if you wish, behind the scenes, your event is your event. Having expertise with and contacts for many of the various locations [insert locations here], our award-winning chef and staff will deliver beyond your expectations.

As you have already seen and tasted, we at ABC offer wine and cheese pairings for the first course, served by a knowledgeable staff. In the past, the tastings and commentary have always pleased our guests, as have literature and reference web sites made available to all guests and included in the gift bag, if desired. Just let us know your specific requirements and we will work with you to impress and make the evening a memorable event.

Sincerely,

Your name

Contact information in smaller form

The Unsolicited Letter

Not having the advantage of knowing who your potential client may be, you must cast a wider net in the unsolicited letter. Not ruling out anything while still letting others know what exactly you do can be difficult. Dressed-up generalities work best in this type of writing. The unsolicited letter often takes the form of a mass-mailing advertisement or a yellow pages/web site ad. Aside from the basics, such as contact information, also found in the solicited letter, this type of letter includes attention-getting content. Let's take a look at a sample ad on page 66.

Advertisements are subjective and sometimes take trial and error. A good rule of thumb is to test them out. What may seem effective to you can seem quite different to someone else. Although friends and family may be easily available, try to find some testers who are "in the business" to some degree and can proof your ad with a more critical eye.

Advertising can be expensive. Here are a few ways to get free advertising for your new or existing company:

- Letters to the editor of your local newspaper
- Volunteering for local organizations (town watch, chamber of commerce, church group, etc.)

ABC Catering

123 Any where Lane
Yourtown, XZ 1000
(123)-555-1212
www.ABCcatering.com

- Pairing wine and food is just one of the things we do
- Weddings, corporate events, family barbeques and more…
- You tell us what you need
- On-or off-site events provided
- No event is too small or large
- Great referrals!

- Giving speeches
- Taking a leadership position in the community

Can you think of any others?

Follow-up to Solicited and Unsolicited Letters

If you are lucky enough to reach the stage where your potential client wishes to know more, that is a very good sign. Being prepared to answer common questions can come in handy at this point. Your answers will depend a lot on your specific organization and locality, but we can make some suggestions to get you started.

Common question #1: "I have never used you before and am a little concerned."
Answer: "We at ABC catering are not new to the business, just a new company made up of experienced individuals with over 20 years in catering."

Common question #2: "The price seems too high."
Answer: "With our exclusive agreements with high-quality vendors, some of the price is passed on to the client; however we believe that your guests will appreciate how unique our events are."

Common question #3: "Aren't all caterers the same?"
Answer: "By no means. With our experienced and knowledgeable staff, we offer more than just hot food and cold drinks—we offer an experience."

THE PROPOSAL

Now, the client almost ready to commit and plans having been discussed, comes the proposal stage, where the outline of the event is put into writing. Although each event will vary, let's look at a sample on the following page.

After the proposal stage, comes the contractual stage. We leave contract writing and interpretation to those in the legal profession.

ABC Catering Logo

Date

Mrs. Kara Krall
123 Anywhere Lane
Philadelphia, PA 19000

Dear Mrs. Krall,

Thank you for considering ABC catering for your daughter's rehearsal dinner on May 16th at 8 p.m. at your residence. We are happy to provide the following:

Butlered Hors D'Oeuvres

Imported cheese and fruit tray—$36 per tray
Grilled Pacific salmon tray—$45 per tray
Assorted (beef, veal, shrimp) puff pastry tray—$38

Main Course

Roasted duck with wild rice
Honey-glazed carrots
Tossed salad

Grilled halibut and country potatoes
Green beans with bacon
Tomato with mozzarella and basil salad
$23 per person

Beverage Service

While sodas and other nonalcoholic drinks will be served at cost, all imported wine will be priced on a per case basis. Spirits will be provided by the client.

Service Cost

8 servers are needed @ $11 per hour

We look forward to making this event a memorable one. If anything else is required or needs to be changed, please let me know.

Sincerely,

FOLLOW-UP LETTER

Now that the event is over, you need to write a follow-up letter. The goal of this letter is to thank your client for choosing you and to tie up any loose ends. Let's look at another example.

ABC Catering Logo

Date

Mrs. Kara Krall
123 Anywhere Lane
Philadelphia, PA 19000

Dear Mrs. Krall,

We hope you enjoyed the service and fine food and wine from ABC catering at your daughter's rehearsal dinner. On our behalf, thank you again for choosing us.

ABC catering believes in serving only the finest food and beverage, with our experienced and knowledgeable staff setting us apart from the rest.

Rehearsal dinners are just one of the many types of events in which we specialize. If we can assist you or someone close to you in their personal of corporate catering needs, just let us know.

Sincerely,

Contact information in smaller form

Summary

Catering organization and makeup differ from company to company. Customer expectations do not—they are always high. Keep in mind that in addition to the photos and gift bags, the written documents that are part of the event are something that endures and may be seen by potential future clients. From start to finish, potential client's questions must be taken into account and your firm's specialty and expertise must be highlighted. Remember, you are hoping to satisfy your current client's needs and do a little marketing for the future as well.

Chapter Questions and Exercises

1. What is the difference between the solicited and the unsolicited marketing letter?
2. What are some points of expertise that a catering organization might highlight?
3. How would they be highlighted?
4. What is a business plan and to whom is it written?
5. What is the goal of the follow-up letter?

Key Terms

- Target market
- Forecasting
- Business plan
- Solicited letter
- Unsolicited letter
- Proposal
- Follow-up letter

5 | ROOMS DIVISION

Richard Sperry has just been informed that he is to take over the responsibilities and duties of the lodging/rooms division because the current manager is leaving. His assignment is provisional while upper-level management considers whether to promote him to the position or open a search for a replacement. Richard had been the assistant manager for over a year and had done well in his last performance review. His duties in the past mostly included interactions with guests and staff on the front line rather than behind-the-scenes management. Most of his time had been spent at the front desk monitoring the check-in and check-out process and coordinating with housekeeping and the other departments on daily needs. He really had no idea what his boss did back in the office. However, he knew he had to familiarize himself with the rooms division manager's duties and began to dig in. While looking through the past manager's files, he encountered folder after folder of documents. "So this is what he did all day while we were out front," he thought to himself. His next thought was that it was now up to him to do the same if he wanted the promotion. Was he up to the task?

Introduction

Rooms division documents deal with a variety of issues and are addressed to guests, co-workers, or external companies. They must often be more concise than that of other departments due to the need to communicate quickly. Getting the message across in a direct and professional manner is key. Writing in the front office primarily takes four forms: memos, logs, messages, and letters. We will look at them one at a time.

MEMOS

More often than not documents for internal use take the form of memos that are meant for members of the staff, co-workers, and superiors. They can cover many areas, from new policies for the check-in process to safety and security alerts. First is an example of a memo to staff regarding billing of guest charges to a corporate account.

What has this memo accomplished? Memos such as these are an important part of any manager's duties, so let's make sure they cover the basics. Generally, memos are

---

ABC Hotel Company

Memo

To: All Front Office Staff

From: Front Office Manager, *JH*

CC: Rooms Division Manager

Date: February 27, 20xx

Re: Corporate Credit Cards

Due to the increase in corporate credit cards being declined during the check-in process, we have contacted the various companies involved and have educated them on our hotel's new policies. If a corporate credit card is declined during the check-in process, it is now required that a personal credit card or cash be used to secure the room.

Please communicate to guests that we at ABC Hotel have notified their respective companies of the new policies and need to implement this new policy to secure payment for the room. If necessary, the front-office manager or manager on duty may be contacted to handle any disputes.

Thank you for your attention to this matter, and do not hesitate to contact me with any questions.

---

used to communicate a particular message to a targeted number of people. Often memos are posted behind the front desk so that all of the staff will see them. A successful memo needs to include the following:

- A clearly written summary of the particular situation
- An indication that superiors have received a copy
- A course of action that is to be undertaken

We assume that the memo was posted behind the front desk, so we assume all staff have seen it. Often hospitality managers require their posted memos to be initialed by staff as proof they have read it. Has our memo accomplished the other tasks? The memo *is* written clearly and concisely. The superior is copied, and finally, the memo offers a plan of action through the manager on duty or the front-office manager, if necessary, so it satisfies that task as well.

Now that we have covered memos to subordinates, let's take a look at memos that have to communicate "up" to superiors or to co-workers. Here is an example.

In communicating with our co-workers and superiors we face the problem of not being their boss. Although most communication in the workplace is not authoritarian, in this situation you must make sure that you do not give orders when writing to these audiences.

ABC Hotel Company

Memo

To: All Front-Line Managers

From: Jeff Heim, Front Office Manager, *JH*

CC: Bart Bartlett, General Manager

Date: September 23, 20xx

Re: Management Computer Training

With the switchover to our new property management system in two months, our vendor will be offering training on the new software. There are many benefits that the new system offers over what we have in place today. There are also many differences that will require you and your staff to be trained on this vital hotel software.

Our vendor estimates that it will take 3 hours per staff member in the

<u>Front office</u>

<u>Reservations</u>

<u>Housekeeping</u>

departments to learn the software; the remaining departments will need to allocate only 2 hours per staff member.

Managers will need a full day of training regardless of department.

I will be contacting you all individually to set up a schedule for you and your staff. Thank you for setting aside the time for this important training.

You are either working with or for the audience of your memo. With that in mind, let's examine the basics of "across-and-up" memos to see how the following criteria are met:

- A clearly identified and presented subject
- A specific audience
- An indication that a superior received a copy of the memo
- Writing that gets across the subject's importance

Has this memo met the criteria? Let's start at the beginning. The subject matter has been presented clearly and in good summary form. The target audience is front-line management, so that criterion has been satisfied. The general manager is copied, so the audience knows that he or she will see it. Finally, the memo appears to be written in a way that communicates the importance of the new software to daily activities, so we can check off the last point as well.

Memos are meant to be direct and concise. Often this brevity can make them seem too direct or cold. Whoever your audience is, get your point across professionally, no matter how brief.

LOGS

More so than memos, logs make up the permanent record of the front office and housekeeping departments in the form of a large, dated book with a sturdy (often leather) cover. The log book is meant to endure physically; its records are meant to as well. In this section we will examine the writing done in the log book by fully staffed shifts and the night audit shift. As with memos, management often requires that all staff initial each log to prove they have read it.

Fully staffed shifts are those from 7 a.m. to 3 p.m. and from 3 p.m. to 11 p.m. (the second shift). The writing in the log book often concerns atypical events and issues requiring special attention and follow-up. The log also serves as a way for the various staff and managers in the front office and housekeeping departments during the first two shifts to communicate with one another. The writing is often brief and needs to cover the basics: Who, What, Where, When, Why.

Let's look at an example from the housekeeping log:

Tuesday July 7, 2009

Room 202 requested a cot be delivered to her room. It was explained to her that one could be provided, however it costs extra.

Upon reading this in the log, a team member or manager would be apprised of the situation but that's all. More detail is needed. A better notation would be the following:

6:30 p.m.

Team member—John P

Room 202 requested that a cot be delivered to her room. It was explained to her that the hotel would be happy to accommodate the room occupant, Mrs. Johnson, however there would be an additional charge of $25.00. Mrs. Johnson stated that she would consider it. Message was left at 7:30 by myself asking if she was still interested.

The situation is spelled out more clearly in this example. More important accountability and follow-up are detailed. This is the most important function of logs: They do not just record the event or request, they also show which member of the hotel staff handled the matter. A night manager who might receive an angry phone call from room 202 wondering where her cot was now has the information with which to handle the situation appropriately.

Deciding which events or requests need to be logged is often a judgment call. A good rule of thumb is to record atypical events, guest complaints, or situations that require follow-up from the next shift.

The front office night audit shift, from 11 p.m. to 7 a.m., often has its own log book detailing any financial matters that warrant logging. Since this shift is responsible for such matters as posting revenue to rooms, departmental totals for that day, and guest charges, among other tasks, a separate book is often used.

Let's look at a typical night audit log entry.

Tuesday July 7, 2009

3:30 a.m.

Team member Bob—night auditor

We continue to see an increase in movie charges being disputed by guests. Total disputes for the day equal 27. This is the highest number I have seen in some time and may be an indication of a problem with our pay-per-view system. I have left messages with both maintenance and the front office and will give an update tomorrow night

7:30 a.m.

Team member Bob—night auditor

Upon speaking with the Front Office Manager, Mike, this morning, it was decided that Mike would look into the situation personally.

This log establishes and links ownership of the situation. If all log entries are handled in this fashion, communication between shifts is done effectively and the guests are better served.

MESSAGES

Messages can take many forms and be addressed to many different parties. In this section we discuss the different types of effectively written messages to guests and colleagues.

To Guests

Understanding that you are a representative of the hotel is critical when communicating with guests. No matter how well you might know a guest, professionalism is paramount in written communication. Often, written communication to guests in a hotel involves communiqués slid under the door, for example, a message about safety like this one regarding the fire alarm.

ABC Hotel Company

12/12/09

Dear Guest,

In our continuing effort to make sure that your stay continues to be a safe one, we will be conducting routine tests of our fire alarm this coming Wednesday, the 13th of December, during the hours between 2 and 4 in the afternoon. If you are present at this time, both our siren and lights will be tested. Again, this is a routine test required by law for your safety. If you should have any questions, please do not hesitate to ask.

Sincerely,

Paul Howard
General Manager

To Colleagues

In addition to memos and logs, another way to communicate to co-workers in writing is through electronic mail (e-mail). A word of caution: If you are using a corporate e-mail account, know that it is not your property. The account is owned by and is the property of your employer. Individuals often assume—incorrectly—that they are the owners of e-mail written at work. But according to the law, this is not the case. Another note of caution: Messages deleted from your computer still exist on your company's e-mail server and the law requires that they be kept there for some time.

With these cautions in mind, we can say that e-mail includes many of the elements and follows many of the same rules as memos and messages. What is often forgotten are the basic rules of grammar that we discussed in Chapter 1.

Whatever form your communication to your co-workers takes, some things to keep in mind are the following:

Your audience may not work for you, but rather with or above you.

Your audience may be at a different location.

Your audience may not be familiar with the specifics or inner workings of your department.

Summary

Front office written communication can take many forms. As we have seen, rooms division managers may create or encounter many different types of writing in their day-to-day work. There is a different set of criteria for writing to staff than to co-workers and guests. But what all forms of communication have in common is that they require professionalism, particularly when addressing guests. Memos are used to announce new policies or concerns, and logs record items for all shifts to see. Finally, messages, whether electronic or written, need to meet the same criteria as memos and logs, and all forms of writing must communciate the subject clearly.

Chapter Questions and Exercises

1. What are some features of a well-written memo?

2. What purpose does a log book serve?

3. Who owns e-mail?

4. Why does the night audit shift often have its own log book?

Key Terms

- Memo
- Log

- Night audit
- Messages

CHAPTER

6 | FOOD AND BEVERAGE

Diana Heim is a food and beverage manager for a busy hotel, The Metropolitan. She's charged with ensuring that all outlets are managed efficiently and effectively. As with many hotels, there are several food and beverage outlets within the one property: a fine-dining gourmet restaurant, banquet rooms, a casual theme restaurant, a night club, room service, snack areas and concession stands, and an employee cafeteria and break rooms. She is also responsible for ensuring that all concession machines (both inside the guest rooms and those located at various places around the hotel) are stocked.

Diana's job involves twenty-four hour, seven-days-a-week activity. She must consolidate orders, limit waste and spoilage, and rotate stock. Communication is crucial for her to stay abreast of all that is happening. Diana has learned that clear, concise, understandable writing is one key to staying in touch with employees and the administration, ensuring procedures, and making seamless transitions from one day to the next, as well as keeping track of the annual calendar of events.

Whether you are running a complex set of food and beverage outlets like Diana, or a small, independent restaurant, written communication is as important as verbal communication in staying on top of what is happening. This chapter covers checklists, notices, memos, invitations, log books, announcements, flyers, and menus—all elements of writing for the food and beverage department.

Introduction

This chapter includes information on the many tasks of writing that befall the food and beverage department. Like most departments, the food and beverage department disperses information to other departments. Clarity and precision in writing is crucial. The ability to disseminate directions and the ability to understand departmental code words and acronyms is central to the success of the food and beverage department.

Food and beverage departments frequently employ the largest numbers of employees. Many food and beverage operations offer 24/7 service: menus change, codes must be enforced, and orders are placed on one shift and arrive during another. Employees are often coming and going—in many food and beverage outlets shifts are staggered, so communications are important and necessary to ensure a smooth operation.

Several key communications procedures that affect the machinery of a efficient and effective operation are discussed in this chapter, including checklists, directions, notices, postings and announcements, letters, directions, log books, and menus.

CHECKLISTS

There is no end to the checklists required for food and beverage. They are the backbone to ensuring consistency in product delivery. No one can know his or her job so well that a checklist becomes unnecessary. Furthermore, food and beverage has one of the highest rates of employee turnover, so checklists help in training. Checklists save time and money. It is the basic nature of checklists to keep people on track.

Checklists also document work that has been completed. They are used as evidence in a legal case and aid in performance evaluations. Checklists used to check or service equipment should always provide space for date, time, and signature. Checklists for opening and closing duties or cleaning lists should have a space for initialling individual items. Other checklists may not require a signature. For example, a manager may have an overall checklist of items to be covered before the dining room opens each night. The skeleton checklist is the same for each shift, but there is space to jot down details.

Checklists are handy tools for communicating "how-to" information to employees. A book of checklists (in plastic covers) should be kept handy at the service station for easy reference. For instance, this book could include a step-by-step procedure for turning on the espresso or cappuccino machine or how to serve cheese. Employees appreciate having easy access to basic information.

The following pages provide examples of checklists for food and beverage outlets. These checklists can be used as a template for any further postings. (*Note*: The Training Program checklist provided in the appendix to this book is a good model for the training of new employees.)

MANAGER CHECKLIST

PREOPENING MEETING

    Staff check
        Time
        Clocked in

    Information sheets to be handed out to staff
        Review details

    Captain assigned
        Confirm details with kitchen

Tables assigned
    Diagram

Specials
    Food
    Drink

Review of duties divided among staff

BANQUET CHECKLIST

DINING ROOM

   Napkin fold
   Linen
   Skirting
   Table numbers
   Glasses polished
   Ice
   Floral arrangements
   Salt and pepper shakers
   Creamers
   Caddies with sugar & sugar substitutes
   Checklist
   Side stations
   Water pitchers
   Coffee/tea station
   Lemons

BAR SET-UP

   Wine:
      White iced
      Red opened

   Beer:
      Iced
      Domestic
      Imports
      Draft
   Bar towels
   Ice
   Glassware
   Stirrers/straws, fruit
   Napkins

KITCHEN SET-UP

   Lemons
   Butter
   Desserts cut
   Garnishes

CHECKLIST FOR CHEESE SERVICE

☑ Bring out cheese from refrigerator about one hour before use.

☑ Arrange the cheeses so that there is a variety of shapes, colors, and flavors. Decorate with celery, walnuts, grapes, apples, radishes, etc.—don't swamp the cheese.

☑ Use a large surface so each cheese can keep its flavor and crumbs apart from the others.

☑ Use a separate knife for blue cheeses.

☑ Use a fork to pick up cheeses.

☑ When cutting a whole cheese, a horizontal slice should be taken, leaving the top surface as even as possible. Scooping cheese is wasteful.

☑ Wedges should be cut lengthwise from nose to cruets. Never cut across the nose of the wedge.

☑ Remove pieces of cheese that have become so small that they are unappealing.

☑ Provide the customer with a clean side plate, side knife (and sometimes fork), and a fresh dish of butter. Cruets should be available. Crackers, toast points, bread, celery, radishes, and fruit may be offered or left on the table.

ORDER OF SERVICE

A. Table seated.

B. Bread service.

C. Take order.

D. First course
1. Sweep.
2. Serve on the left with the left hand.
3. Check water and/or beverages.
4. Clear course and utensils used.
5. Remove used drink glasses.
6. Clear from the right with the right hand.

E. Second course
7. Sweep.
8. Check water and beverages.
9. Brew coffee/prepare back station for coffee/tea service.
10. Clear course and utensils.

F. Entrée
11. Sweep.
12. Check water and beverages.
13. Clear course and utensils.
14. Crumb tables.
15. Remove everything from the tables that will not be used (i.e., salt and pepper shakers, unused silverware, and butter plates. The only thing left on the table after this course is a spoon (if unused) and beverage glass that is still being used.

G. Dessert/Coffee
16. Replenish silverware.
17. Serve all tables, pouring coffee from the right with the right hand. Use a guard when pouring coffee.
18. Serve dessert from the left with the left hand.
19. Clear dessert from the right with the right hand.
20. Replenish water and coffee.
21. Clear any and all unnecessary items from the table. All that should be left on the table after the dessert course is cleared is the table decoration, candle, and coffee/tea cup (if the guest is still drinking coffee/tea; otherwise, remove).

H. Chocolates/mints
22. If chocolates are to be served, place on the table.

I. After Dinner Drinks
23. Check your list to see if after-dinner drinks will be offered.

J. Departure
24. Assist and thank guests as they depart.

HOW-TO CHECKLIST FOR FOOD AND BEVERAGE SERVICE

BASIC PATTERN OF SERVICE

The basic model for service is:

- Appetizer
- Soup
- Salad
- Entrée
- Coffee
- Dessert

HOW-TO CHECKLIST FOR POURING DRINKS

PERFECTING THE PROPER POUR

- Before the first drop is served, ensure that all glassware is sparkling. Do not use stained coffee cups.

- Serve drinks at the correct temperature. Prewarm pots if they are used and serve only fresh tea and coffee. Don't pour iced drinks into a glass still warm from the dishwasher.

- Do not overfill pots or individual glasses—it only makes it difficult to pour out or drink from them.

- Avoid picking up glassware or cups to fill. Do not pour water from the side of the pitcher.

- Serve from the right with the right hand. Put drinks to the right side of customers or directly in front if they are not having food. A handle should always be at 5 o'clock.

- Look out for left-handed customers. They will be pleasantly surprised if you put their drinks on the left side.

- If a customer would like a fresh cup of coffee and the first, only half-drunk cup, has gone cold, offer a clean cup.

- When placing pitchers, jugs, or pots of liquids on the table, the handles should point toward the customer. Put sugar bowls, milk, cream, etc. within easy reach.

- When a customer requests water, ask the others at the table whether they would also like some.

- When serving bottled waters, pour some in each glass at the table, and then place the bottle on the table with the label facing the person who ordered it. Seve bottled water chilled, but without ice, because ice cubes are made from different water. Serve ice cubes if requested.

- If a customer produces his or her own tea bag and requests a pot of hot water, oblige with a sincere smile. There may be health reasons why the guest must stick to a specific tea.

ELEMENTS OF SERVICE

- Expect that your guests will want all the courses, but don't act disappointed if they do not order all of them.

- Whatever a guest's reasons for ordering or not ordering, be polite and do not judge.

- Service for each of the courses is similar.

- Remember to take away any used flat-ware and replenish whatever the guest will be using for the next course before the course is placed on the table.

- Crumb the table—not between each course, but after the entrée is cleared and after dessert if necessary.

- Some guests like to have coffee with the dessert; some prefer it after. You can still set all the coffee cups at the same time, with the cup handles at five o'clock, and pour the coffee whenever the guest wants it.

THE DINING ROOM SHOWCASE

- Showcase the dining room at all times.
- Refold and replace napkins when the guest has left the table.
- Be in the dining room at all times when the station is occupied regardless of table status.
- Be aware of all tables, not just your assigned tables.
- Never scrape plates in the dining room.
- Remove all glassware by the stem and plates by the edge.
- Use a tray to remove more than one glass.
- Follow mise-en-place at all times. All that should remain at the conclusion of the meal is the beverage being consumed.
- Keep your hands to your sides or behind your back and always still.
- Speak directly to your guest using eye contact. Your conversation with a guest should not be audible to another table.
- Consolidate your tasks.
- Never leave the dining room empty-handed.
- Show a sense of urgency.
- Realize you are getting into the weeds before it is too late and be professional enough to ask for help.
- Assist and thank guests as they depart.

CHECKLIST TO OPEN HONEYBAKED HAM & CAFÉ

- ☑ Run Mgr. Report #7 to make sure the balance is zero. If not, follow instructions on the front page in the Aspect folder in the office.
- ☑ Take register and credit card reports to the back office.
- ☑ Put credit card report in accountant's folder along with bank deposit when you get it.
- ☑ Run the **daily sales report** from the Aspect program on the computer.
- ☑ Staple the nightly reports (#7 and #8) to the **daily sales report** along with any paid outs to the left-hand side. The credit card slips get clipped to the right-hand side. File in the Monthly Reports folder.
- ☑ Unlock safe and return the money from the envelopes to the drawers according to the corresponding numbers on each.
- ☑ Take drawers to the front.
- ☑ Check temperatures on all coolers, pull bread and meat as needed, and check for anything that you may need to get at the store for the day.
- ☑ Go to the bank and, if necessary, grocery store.

NOTICES

Notices also help to "get the word out" quickly. They are meant to be loud and, well, noticeable.

Notices can serve a variety of purposes and are not limited, of course, to the food and beverage department. Notices routinely posted are warnings, announcements, and advertisements. Two common types of notices are the sign and the poster.

Warnings

Examples of ineffective warnings:

- *On a dessert box:* Do not turn upside down (printed on the bottom of the box).
- *On a pack of peanuts:* Instructions: open packet, eat nuts.
- *Warning to staff:* For safety reasons all staff and students are reminded that the taking of hot drinks out of the fast-food areas is strictly forbidden.

  Several slipping accidents have already occurred as a result of liquid being spilt on the floor, and the probability of someone suffering from a serious scalding accident while walking along busy corridors and getting into crowded lifts is high.

  Your full cooperation in ensuring that you do not put yourself and others at risk is required. (Stated more simply, this would be: Open drinks outside the employee cafeteria are strictly forbidden. A famous legal case involving hot coffee resulted in McDonalds printing the following on its coffee cups: "Warning—Contents may be hot.")

Warnings are best when they contain a visual image and few words. Signage can be purchased to serve your needs.

Announcements

Announcements are used for a variety of purposes. They keep both customers and employees in the loop. They can make a statement or declare or convey a message. You might use announcements to post news of engagements, births, promotions, high sales, employee of the month, and so forth. Typically, announcements share good information, though they might also be required to post news of closings or job openings. In general, announcements provide public information.

Example:

JOB ANNOUNCEMENT: COOK
Paddy's Restaurant
$10.00–$11.50 Hourly (DOE)
APPLICATIONS ACCEPTED: December 15 through March 15, 20XX

Enhance your cooking experience
Are you a motivated individual?
Do you enjoy serving and working with the public?

Paddy's Restaurant team is committed to providing excellent service to our guests and a positive and upbeat working environment to our staff.

If you are an enthusiastic, energetic individual who has strong interpersonal skills and enjoys being part of a team, we would be interested in hearing from you!

Paddy's Restaurant.......Come work where you play!

Responsibilities:
- Cook is under immediate supervision of the Executive Chef.
- Performs a variety of operations and related tasks in support of food and beverage services for Paddy's Restaurant guests, events and/or activities.
- Responsibilities include preparing and serving a variety of menu items with an attractive plate presentation and in a friendly manner.
- Must be capable of taking direction as well as exercising self-motivation in keeping the kitchen and dining areas clean, rotating food products daily and working at a pace that allows for minimal guest waiting times.

This position may also assist with or is assigned the following duties:

- Provide excellent guest services to internal and external guests.
- Properly cook and prepare foods and beverages as required by menus, ensuring that items are correctly portioned.
- Assure that all items are available by thinking ahead and anticipating demand.
- Assure that the kitchen and dining areas are kept clean and are well maintained.
- Assist in the inspection of the kitchen to see that it is equipped with necessary supplies.
- Safely clean cooking equipment and work areas to maintain sanitary safety and healthful conditions.
- Sweep floors and wipe down counters; may wash dishes and empty trash.
- Perform end-of-shift assignments such as cleaning counter equipment and surfaces with a bleach solution, filtering deep fryers and emptying and thoroughly cleaning all grease containers.
- Perform daily tasks as required by weekly cleaning schedule.
- Operate standard cooking equipment such as bake ovens, stoves, fryers, toasters, food slicer.
- Perform routine maintenance and cleaning.
- Clean all equipment using proper procedures.
- Perform special projects and other duties as assigned from time to time.

Minimum Qualifications

Previous cooking experience is highly desired but not required.

Closing Date

This position will remain open until filled.

Where to Apply

Paddy's Restaurant
Human Resources Division, Room 110
65 Restaurant Way
St. Paul, MN 55117

http://www.paddy'srestaurant/human_resorces/jobs

Paddy's Restaurant IS AN EQUAL OPPORTUNITY EMPLOYER

Example:

Call For Nominations—Employee of the Month
** It's time for selection of the employee of the month. **

Please send the following information to Katie Price by 5:00 p.m. on Wednesday, November 15, 20xx:

- Nominated employee's name
- Nominated employee's department
- Your name
- Your title
- Your department

In two or three sentences, state why you believe the said employee is eligible for the Employee of the Month Award.

Example:

Announcement

Employee of the Month Winners

The Unique Hotel Employee of the Month winner for September was **Patricia Marie Smith**. Patricia was chosen for **Outstanding Customer Service**. She is a restaurant server in the **Department of Food and Beverage**.

Comments made about Ms. Smith included: "Patricia has set new high standards for customer service in the department of food and beverage. She is always on time and considerate of others and provides exceptional service to all guests. If at all possible, she works with others to ensure the smooth operation of the dining room. She is an excellent mentor to new employees and is always available to help others. Patricia takes great pride in her work and sets the standard for others to follow."

Patricia received a $100 gift certificate, commemorative plaque, and automatic nomination for the Employee of the Year. Patricia donated her gift to the local high school culinary class.

Example:

Announcement of New Vendor

Monday, August 18, 20xx

Food and Beverage Operations Announces New Contracts
for Vending Machines and Coffee

On August 14th an announcement was made to department heads that The University of State entered into contracts with ALPHA Food Services for vending machine and coffee services. Brand-new beverage and snack vending machines will be located at the Student Complex on Monday, August 23rd. Under the contractual relationship with ALPHA, coffee services for the student meeting rooms and dormitory kitchens will be handled through a centralized process, managed by Food and Beverage Operations.

We believe that the new process will provide students with better pricing, efficiency, and services. The term "coffee services" can be used interchangeably with kitchen supplies and includes items such as coffee, tea, sweetener, creamer, etc.

A web site with Frequently Asked Questions as well as locations of the vending machines and departmental kitchens has been developed and can be accessed at: http://www.studentservices.edu.

Example:

Classes Offered to Employees

Yoga Classes for Employees

Yoga classes will be offered to all employees and significant others. Be sure to sign up before the starting date.

Starting Date:
Wednesday, February 16, 20XX

Time:
12:00 noon to 1:00 p.m. in ASH 9 Board Room

Interested in joining Yoga?

Contact:
Beth Millemann at bethm@yogaisforme.edu

Remember:
You can also find the weekly newsletter archived on the web site: Employee Services News Archive (http://www.yourinformationhere.htm).

INVITATIONS

Responsibility for invitations to various events often falls under the responsibility of the department of food and beverage. Having a creative cache of invitations in your files can help attract people to your services and alleviate the worries of guests.

Invitations are used for any number of events: weddings, birthdays, graduations, private parties, holiday events, and so much more. You name it, and there is an invitation to be prepared.

Invitations should include the following information:

- Who is throwing the party and who the party is honoring
- What the celebration is
- Date
- Location
- When (date, time)
- RSVP telephone number, e-mail

LOG BOOKS

A communications log book is essential to any food and beverage department. Because many food and beverage departments are 24/7 operations, a log book helps to streamline communication and document what occurred during any specific shift.

Simply put, log books save time. The first thing any manager in food and beverage should do when arriving for a shift is to read the log book from the previous shift. Likewise, the last thing the manager should do is write down for the next person on duty all important activities performed during that shift.

As we all know, turnover in food and beverage is higher than in other departments. Log books can serve as a review for a new manager. For example, reading what par levels were required the previous week, month, or year can save time and money, not to mention provide assurance.

Log books can be as simple as a composition book. They should be chained (literally) to the food and beverage office desk so that they don't get lost, for when several managers use the same office and same desk, it is easy for things to go astray. Clipboards are also helpful in keeping track of office communication.

Log books should start with the date and time. Entries should be kept relatively simple and pointed. Following the simple flow of the day's activities helps to communicate what happened that day, special interests, things to do, on-the-job injuries, commendations, deposits made, and orders placed. It is important to write clearly (or print) the information so that anyone can read and understand.

FLYERS

Flyers are like announcements, but less wordy. Flyers can be posted for any number of reasons. A good flyer is one that is easily visible and contains only the information necessary to get the message across simply.

Flyers should point people in the direction they need to take to get further information. For example, the Sodexho flyer announcing internships is clear and concise and provides just enough information to entice someone to go to the next level. Details are not necessary at this point. The idea is to attract attention . . . to intrigue.

Chapter Questions and Exercises

1. Create checklists for your own department. What are the step-by-step details that need to be included?
2. Why is it important for food and beverage employees to communicate clearly?
3. What notices are necessary within the food and beverage department?
4. Name five creative ways to attract guests to your restaurant. A party?
5. How do banquet managers communicate with other departments within a hotel?
6. Create a log book for a food and beverage department. What headings are needed? Where would you place the log book? When would managers write in the log book and when would they read it? Is it necessary for others, aside from managers, to read or write in the log book? If so, who?

Key Terms

- Checklists
- Notices
- Announcements
- Invitations
- Log books
- Flyers

CHAPTER

7 | TECHNOLOGY

Richard Sperry knew that it was time to replace the point-of-sale system in his restaurant when it continued to crash day after day, often during the busy periods. The existing system was about ten years old and was fairly easy to use, according to his staff. However, it was breaking down too much and management had given him the go-ahead and funds to purchase a new system. After a little research, Richard found out quickly that there were many options available on the market. Knowing that he had some research and site visits ahead of him, he got lucky and received a template for a Request for Proposal (RFP), a document that is sent out to potential vendors when you are interested in purchasing a system, from a former colleague and knew that much of the work was already done for him. He merely had to "tweak" it to suit his business. If he could do this in the right way, using this RFP could really simplify his search considerably.

INTRODUCTION

RFPs can make a business manager's life a lot easier. The goal is to get vendors to answer your specific questions in writing while describing for them the specifics and needs of your business. RFPs are used when the item or service to be purchased is large and intricate—for example, computer solutions such as a point-of-sale systems (POS). Here is the template used by a fictional hotel that is sending out an RFP to various vendors who sell POS; it begins with the table of contents, which explains its layout.

XYZ Property

Point-of-Sale RFP

*Proposals in response to this Request for Proposal (RFP)
are due by close of business on ....*

CONFIDENTIALITY STATEMENT

This document, its enclosures, attachments and all other information, spoken or written, made available in regard to any information herein, are confidential and proprietary property of The XYZ property. Any disclosure or reproduction of the above-referenced information in a verbal, written, photographed, photocopied, electronic or other manner, without prior written consent of an officer of XYZ property, is prohibited. Even then, those so authorized may only use the information consistent with the consent and only for purposes of addressing the goals, objectives, and requirements contained within this document. All copies of any portion of this document must include this Confidentiality Statement.

Extreme care should be taken in the methods and locations used to review, discuss, and store this document. By receiving this document you assume full responsibility as outlined in this Confidentiality Statement and agree to be bound by all interpretations thereof. Unauthorized disclosure of the information contained herein as described above, or as a result of eavesdropping of any type, will be your sole responsibility and punishable by the fullest extent allowable by law.

TABLE OF CONTENTS

I   INTRODUCTION

A. Scope

Property XYZ is seeking a feature-rich Point-of-Sale System (POS) that will support the operational requirements for the food & beverage outlets as defined in this Request for Proposal (RFP). This RFP provides the necessary information for you to prepare a proposal and also provides background information about XYZ. The purpose of the RFP is to effect the successful negotiation, execution, and consummation of a definitive agreement between Property XYZ and appropriate bidder(s) to provide XYZ with a Point-of-Sale System.

B. Objectives

To select a full-featured POS System that will address not only the standard POS requirements but also the many unique operational needs of a full-service resort like XYZ. At a minimum, the final solution must:

- Provide a quick, simple, and straightforward solution for entering and tendering guest checks using touch-screen technology.
- Be a user-friendly system that is easy to learn and requires minimal training.
- Provide management with effective controls for day-to-day management.
- Provide comprehensive, timely, and accurate information.
- Provide comprehensive and flexible reporting and inquiry capabilities.
- As much as possible, XYZ would like to maintain a paperless system for record keeping.
- Function using hand-held devices for all pool-side outlets.
- Provide operational flexibility to meet the day-to-day challenges and procedural adjustments typical of a new opening.
- Be fully functional with all staff properly trained by opening day.

Although price is an important factor in this process, XYZ places great importance on the quality and dependability of the products reviewed. To determine the quality of systems proposed, emphasis will be placed on the following factors:

- Stability and soundness of the programs (i.e., full-featured, robust, and proven reliability)
- System integrity and security
- The vendor's reputation for quality hardware, software, and service with existing customers

C. Property Overview

[Insert as much detail about your property here. Include physical layout, number on staff, target market, etc.] For our purposes, XYZ is a restaurant in a 500-room hotel with a pool and golf course. Management also runs a second hotel that needs a POS in its restaurant.

D. Project Schedule

The following dates reflect an estimated time frame for POS selection, contract negotiation, and installation for the vendor's use in planning responses. This information is subject to change by XYZ.

DATES	ACTION
5/27/200x	RFP Sent to Vendors
6/17/200x	RFP Received Back
7/15/200x	Decision Made by Owners
9/1/200x	Contract Signed
9/13/200x	Equipment Ordered
11/15/200x	Installation and Training site 1
12/15/200x	Grand Opening—site 1
6/1/200x	Equipment Ordered—site 2
8/1/200x	Installation and Training—site 2
10/1/200x	Grand Opening—site 2

E. Bidding Guidelines

The bids and proposals in response to this Request for Proposal should comply with the following guidelines:

1. All areas of consideration must be answered concisely, following the directions outlined under each subheading. All statements must be supported with concrete examples or explanations. Ambiguous statements such as "... all reasonable support" are not acceptable.

2. Vendors who wish to provide information that is not addressed in the RFP are encouraged to do so as an addendum to the proposal. We realize the approach of each potential vendor will be unique. We have therefore attempted to present the specifications in general terms. Points that we feel are essential, however, are presented in detail.

3. Vendors are encouraged to provide any additional information, insight, thoughts, and ideas on how the vendor can help XYZ succeed with this project.

4. XYZ reserves the right to introduce additional factors not contained in this RFP in order to obtain the most suitable solution. After submitting a proposal, each vendor must be prepared to have the operational aspects of their proposed system reviewed in detail by XYZ representatives. A portion of this review may be requested without vendor presence.

5. Questions regarding any information herein should be directed to the project manager from XYZ. **Vendors must not contact any XYZ employees directly.**

6. Vendors judged to be the most qualified to fulfill XYZ's requirements will be invited to visit for further discussions. This meeting will include a demonstration of the proposed system. At this time, each bidder must be prepared to elaborate upon and clarify its written proposal.

7. XYZ plans to make their initial selection within 30–45 days following the final vendor demonstration meeting.

8. Failure to comply with any of the RFP response requirements may subject a proposal to rejection.

9. **Each vendor must be prepared to include any or all statements made in their proposal in a contract for systems and services, or as an addendum to that**

contract. Acceptance of proposals from any source in no way obligates XYZ to the vendor. Furthermore, such acceptance is not a guarantee of any type for current or future business relations. XYZ reserves the right to accept or reject any and all proposals, in whole or in part, at any time.

10. Each proposal must be signed by a duly authorized officer of the submitting company.
11. Two (2) copies of the response to this RFP must be received at the project manager's office, one (1) hard copy along with one (1) soft copy, by the date on the cover of this document. Refer to the cover page for complete address information.
12. Any vendor selected to provide systems to XYZ will be required to present an insurance certificate as proof of liability covering the full scope of their work, for at least $1,000,000.
13. Each vendor submitting a proposal must be a direct national representative of the manufacturer, or the actual manufacturer. (If you elect to submit the RFP through your local dealer, please specify the name, address, and number of the dealer chosen to service XYZ.)
14. XYZ requires that vendors provide access, via a software escrow agent, to any applicable software source code, in the event that vendor is no longer able to provide effective support or to continue enhancing the product. Please indicate how this would need to be handled.
15. XYZ reserves the right to adjust the Project Schedule dates at its sole discretion.
16. The vendor's costs for proposal preparation, demonstration, and testing will be the sole responsibility of the vendor.

II   VENDOR INFORMATION

The following information must be supplied by each vendor:

A. General Information
Respond to all questions detailed in "Appendix A—Vendor Questionnaire."

B. Financial
Provide a copy of your latest annual report or audited financial statements including the balance sheet, income statement, and statement of cash flow. As with all information in your response, this data will be held in confidence. Please note that a "call my banker" response is not acceptable.

C. Experience
Provide a brief background on your company along with major milestones in the company history.

D. References
Provide a list of customers with a similar configuration, preferably local or regional, using the proposed system along with the list of modules currently in use. Please provide at least two of these references for installations completed in the last year. Please also provide a list of similar installations currently in progress.

Please provide the following for each reference.

- Company name
- Company address
- Contact person (management)
- Company telephone number
- Description of system and use
- Date of implementation

E. Literature
Please attach any additional information that describes your product. Describe what is unique about the proposed solution and what sets it apart from other proposals.

III GENERAL REQUIREMENTS

The following areas detail some of the general requirements to be considered in the identification of the new POS for XYZ.

A. Network Operating Environment

While the network operating system will not drive the purchase of the POS system, a graphical user environment (GUI) using Windows XP at the server with Windows XP or Vista at the workstation is the preferred approach. It is critical that vendors should propose the most stable and robust environment with a proven track record for their system. This includes Unix or any form of thin-client. All POS terminal locations will be cabled with either Enhanced Cat-5 twisted pair or fiber (still to be determined). The current plan for connecting the networks at the two locations, the Country Club and the Hotel, includes T3 data communications lines.

Server Configuration

The POS configuration must include the necessary components to ensure that at no time will the system at either location be inoperative in the event of a communications failure between the two locations. For those systems that support continued use of the POS terminal while communication with the server is down, a single server at the hotel is an acceptable configuration. For those that do not, a server will be required at both locations (note "Section E. Consolidated Reporting" for this configuration). The property management system, however, will operate off a single server at the Hotel, and the POS systems at both locations must interface to the PMS.

XYZ will be looking to the vendor for assistance with the hardware and networking requirements, including:

- Providing specifications for all hardware, including terminals, printers, file server, and any other necessary peripherals.
- While XYZ is considering sourcing hardware from a third party, those POS vendors that sell hardware are encouraged to submit hardware prices as well.
- Upon completion of the installation, MIS personnel must be thoroughly trained on all aspects of system maintenance.

B. Device Requirements

Proposed POS terminals should be a PC-based, flat-screen, active-matrix PC POS terminal with integrated credit card reader. They should be durable, environmentally sealed (protected from spills), and as much as possible, scratch resistant. Receipt printers should be thermal for the front-of-house and dot-matrix for the back (for two- color printing). Due to frequent electrical problems in the southern Florida area, surge and UPS protection is critical.

C. Modules

The following POS modules and general functionality are required by XYZ:

- Basic F&B POS functionality in the revenue outlets as defined in "Section IV Functionality Requirements."

- Handheld use for certain outlets.
- Comprehensive package tracking (through interface with the PMS).

XYZ will also require the following modules/applications:

- Restaurant Management System (RMS) to include:
  o Cash management and reporting
  o Management reporting
  o Inventory & purchasing
  o Report generator
- Retail POS for retail outlets

XYZ is also considering the following applications:

- Frequent Diner
- Table Management
- Menu Management
- Restaurant Reservations
- Minibar

NOTE: As outlined above, XYZ will be selecting numerous F&B related applications outside of just POS. We realize all vendors will not be able to propose all applications. At a minimum, interfaces with each of these will be required.

D. Interfaces

A very critical component to the POS system will be the interfacing with other hotel systems. Vendors must clearly define the functionality available with each interface.

Depending on the modules being proposed, the new system must provide the following interfaces. Where applicable, vendors currently being considered are listed. Others may be added or removed as necessary.

For all interfaces listed below, vendors must provide:

- A detailed description of the features and functionality supported by the interface.
- A listing of those systems to which an interface is already available and installed.

Where applicable, the above information should be provided even for those applications being proposed (such as inventory), as XYZ may still decide to purchase the POS System from one vendor and the other system from another.

1. ***Property Management System (PMS).*** Due to the resort nature of XYZ along with the extensive offering of activities and food and beverage, package tracking will be critical. Any systems that offer enhanced interface functionality to include package handling should provide a detailed functionality description. On the average, packages are expected to account for approximately 50% of the daily occupancy.

PMS Vendors currently being considered include:

- Encore
- HSI
- Micros Fidelio
- MAI
- MSI
- Resolutions
- Springer-Miller Systems

LANmark
Jaguar
Version 7.1
HIS

Guest View
SMS|Host

2. ***Credit Card Processing.***   A single credit card processing system to be used property-wide has yet to be determined. The selection of this system will be driven by the selected property management system vendor.

3. ***In-Room Entertainment.***   Interface will be necessary to allow for room service ordering directly through the in-room entertainment system in the guest room. Vendors currently being considered include:
   - LodgeNet
   - On command

4. ***Minibar.***   If an interface is available with any minibar systems, provide system names and functionality.

5. ***Golf Tee Time.***   If an interface is available with any tee-time systems, provide system names and functionality.

6. ***Purchasing/Inventory.***

7. ***Menu Management.***

8. ***Reservations.***

9. ***Table Management.***

10. ***Accounting.***   This applies to an interface with Purchasing.

11. ***Golf Cart GPS.***   Ability to interface with golf cart GPS system to enable food and beverage ordering while on the golf course. Designed to allow food prep prior to arrival between the 9th and 10th holes.

When planning the interface installations, the vendor must:

- Give The XYZ project manager adequate advance notice of all tasks for which the hotel is responsible.
- Vendors must ensure that all interfaces will be up and running on each of the opening dates.
- A permanent backup plan must be in place by go-live so that no postings are lost in the event of a system problem.
- Backup procedures must be detailed in writing.

E. Consolidated Reporting

Due to the unique layout of XYZ, with two separate locations, there are specific reporting requirements that must be supported. Each outlet must be able to report individually, each location must be able to report individually, and consolidated reporting including both locations must also be available.

IV   FUNCTIONALITY REQUIREMENTS

Please respond to all questions in "Appendix B – Functionality Requirements." While completing the questionnaire, keep in mind all information detailed in Sections I through III of this proposal.

For the section on "Tracking and Reporting," report samples should be provided.

For other sections, screen captures should be provided as necessary.

To help us better understand your solution, please feel free to add additional descriptions or details as necessary.

If you are able to supply any of the other modules currently being considered (i.e., table management, menu management, reservations, frequent diner, minibar, or retail POS), please provide functionality descriptions for those modules. Provide any screen captures that may help to describe functionality.

V PROPOSAL FORMAT

All vendors must follow the format described in this section when completing and submitting proposals for consideration. Each section of the proposal must be clearly labeled and separated by an index tab also lettered and labeled as indicated in this section.

A Vendor Information	I Implementation & Training
B Scope of Proposal	J Documentation
C Requirements Matrix	K System Upgrades
D Sample Reports & Screen Layouts	L Contracts
E Operating Environment	M System Costs
F System Response Time	
G Equipment Configuration	
H Physical and Environmental Requirements	

The required sections for vendor responses include the following:

Section A: Vendor Information
This section should consist of the responses to the questions.

Section B: Scope of Proposal
This section of the proposal should be a concise statement of the relevant factors in the vendor's approach to supplying hardware, software, support, and other key elements as each applies to XYZ's requirements and objectives. Briefly describe the proposed system, highlighting major features, functions, and any areas of potential noncompliance with RFP requirements.

State the modules that you are proposing in response to this RFP. Describe the methods that you will use to ensure compatibility with the other systems to which we will be interfacing.

Section C: Functionality Requirements
This section should consist of the completed requirements form in "Appendix B– Functionality Requirements."

Section D: Sample Reports and Screen Layouts
In Section D, include sample reports and screen layouts.

Section E: Operating Environment
Section E should begin with a description of the proposed operating environment, incorporating the requirements. Vendor proposals should describe the specific version of the operating system that would be installed with the proposed system. Indicate how long the vendor applications have been operating on this version of

the operating system in a live environment. In addition, please provide the following information:

> **Languages/Development Tools:**   Indicate the programming languages used to develop your system. State what other tools are used in developing your system.
>
> **Database:**   Describe the file organization/database structure supported by your operating system.

Section F: System Response Time

Based on vendor experience, please indicate the following response times assuming a hotel and f&b configuration similar to XYZ that has been operating and accumulating data for one year:

> **Credit Card Approval:**   Indicate the wait time for a credit card approval from the time of the card swipe assuming your recommended method of data communications is in place.
>
> **Backup:**   Indicate the backup time for daily, weekly, and monthly backups.
>
> **Daily Processing:**   If applicable, indicate the processing time required for the end-of-day process.
>
> **System Startup:**   In the event of a system failure, indicate the time for the system to be up and fully functional from the time the server is powered up.

Section G: Equipment Configuration

In Section E, please detail specific information including itemized cost for *all* of the hardware that you are proposing. If you are not proposing hardware, please indicate the same specifications for equipment that would be required to run your application.

Where applicable, please make sure to include the following information:

> **File Server(s):**   Model number, speed, memory size, hard disk capacity, and configuration. Include size and model of monitor.
>
> **Storage:**   Type (disk, tape), model number, cost, and capacity.
>
> *NOTE:* The new system must include the bidder's recommendation for either hardware redundancy or fault tolerance. If the hardware proposed is to be redundant, the recommended hardware configuration should specify all redundant components and their quantities required for redundancy.
>
> **POS Terminal:**   Model number, speed, memory size, network card, and hard disk capacity. Include size and type of touch-screen monitor along with information about cash drawer.
>
> **Printers:**   Model number(s), speed, size, and required accessories. Please indicate which printers will be connected to the network and those that would be "slave" printers.
>
> **Modems:**   Indicate the number and type of modems necessary for the proposed configuration.
>
> **Other Hardware:**   Please provide the necessary details for any other recommended hardware, including network hubs and uninterrupted power supplies.

Section H: Physical and Environmental Requirements

In this section, present an outline of technical and preinstallation assistance your firm will provide. Also explain what is required but not provided by your company and how it is normally accomplished.

List all site preparation information, including server space requirements, any special mounting methods required, special power requirements (including any need for isolated power circuits), and the number and type of required data communication lines. Please include information on cabling requirements along with electrical, architectural, and other special concerns. Indicate the maximum distance that all peripherals may be located from the computer or control unit.

In addition, describe any environmental requirements for the proposed system, including air-conditioning, humidity control, power supply, etc.

PHASE I			**PHASE II**		
Department	Staff	Management	Department	Staff	Management

Section I: Implementation & Training

The following table details the staff training requirements for each of the two phases: Based on these staffing levels (which only includes staffing numbers for employees that will require system training) and the two opening phases, please provide detailed information on the proposed training process for XYZ, including:

- A sample installation schedule using a calendar without dates.
- Total number of training hours for each phase.
- Number of vendor trainers required for each phase.

Include the recommended number of days for the following:

- Network installation
- Network training for MIS personnel
- Interface installation
- On site post-conversion support

Please also provide the total cost for all implementation and training services outlined above.

Using the following format, summarize the assignments, responsibilities, due dates, and associated costs, where applicable, for implementing the proposed system. Systems must be fully functional on the dates. Add any factors not listed in the implementation schedule that are relevant to a successful implementation, including detailed customer responsibilities.

TASKS	ASSIGNED TO		TIME
	XYZ	VENDOR	

Section J: Documentation

Provide a list of the user and system operating manuals that will be provided. In addition, please include a copy of the table of contents and index for each. Please state if technical writing assistance will be provided to document XYZ-specific policies and procedures relating to your system. This could include any necessary interface procedures, emergency network procedures, and any necessary checklists (such as night audit or front office management procedures). Indicate your policy for documentation of system enhancements or upgrades, how the user base is updated, how often, etc.

Section K: System Upgrades

In this section, please provide the following information regarding software upgrades:

- Are new releases with improved and additional functionality provided on a regular basis? If so, how often?
- How would your company handle system upgrades for an installation of this size?
- What kinds of additional training and implementation services are provided for new releases and at what cost?

Section L: Contracts

In this section, include samples of all contracts related to your proposal. Include hardware, software, service, support, and supplies contracts and any information needed to assess the scope of each.

Section M: System Costs

In this section, please include all costs associated with the project as defined in this RFP. Provide the complete itemized cost for each hardware and software component of the proposed system. Include unit cost, extended cost, quantity discount scales, and total cost for each item. Also indicate the length of time quoted prices are valid.

Please make sure to include the following:

- All applications, modules and interfaces
- Network operating system
- Other required utilities
- Programming: Hourly/daily rate for programmers, consultants and any other individuals who may be necessary if specialty programming is required.
- Installation: Itemize all installation costs
- Other costs: Itemize any other related costs not already listed

Summary

With the many advances and complexities involved in purchasing technology, knowledge of and professional use of a Request for Proposal are required. From the beginning or introduction, where your specific needs, overview, and guidelines are conveyed to the vendor, the RFP gets your information across directly and unambiguously. Next, in the general requirements sections, the RFP lays out your more detailed requirements—in the case illustrated in this chapter, the network layout and the functionality requirements, or what exactly the system is to accomplish. Finally, the purchaser (you) gives vendors the format for their answers. Specifying the answer format makes comparing the many responses easier. Preparing and using a RFP according to these steps will lead to productive purchasing.

Chapter Questions and Exercises

1. What is a RFP and why is it used?
2. What should be covered in each of the five sections?
3. Why is it important to have your potential vendors follow a common format when responding to the RFP?
4. How would the RFP illustrated in the chapter be changed to fit a different department?
5. How would the RFP be changed to fit a different product/service?

Key Terms

- Scope
- Objectives
- Property overview
- Project schedule
- Bidding guidelines
- General information
- Financial
- Experience
- References
- Literature
- Network operating environment

- Device requirement
- Modules
- Interfaces
- Consolidated reporting
- Vendor information
- Scope of proposal
- Functionality requirements
- Sample reports
- Screen layouts
- Operating environment
- System response time
- Equipment configuration

- Physical and environmental requirements
- Implementation and training
- Documentation
- System upgrades
- Contracts
- System costs

Appendix

The following pages contain ten checklists, one for each day of a new employee's training program for the food and beverage department. Both the trainer and the trainee are to sign each line of the daily checklists. The checklists are kept in a file that is accessible to all trainers. The idea here is that no matter who is assigned to train for a particular shift, the trainers can look at the file and know exactly where the new employee is to be in his/her training program.

Day One: . . . . Approximately 2 hours
    Tour of the restaurant
    Introductions to all personnel
    Overview of the training manual
    Overview of the next two weeks of training

Day Two: . . . . Approximately 3 hours
    Introduce menus
    Service style
    Computer systems

Day Three: . . . . Approximately 3 hours
    Wine service/cocktails
    Computer systems

Day Four: . . . . Approximately 5 hours
    Follow a captain
    Beverage service

Day Five: . . . . Approximately 5 hours
    Follow a captain
    Computer programs
    Cocktails

Day Six: . . . . Approximately 5 hours
    Follow a captain
    Table settings
    Buffet

Day Seven: . . . . Approximately 5 hours
    Follow a captain
    Wine service

Day Eight: . . . . Approximately 5 hours
    Take tables under supervision of a captain
    Review beverage service, alcoholic and nonalcoholic drinks

Day Nine: . . . . Approximately 5 hours
    Take tables under the supervision of a captain
    Review menus

Day Ten: . . . . Approximately 5 hours
    Take tables under the supervision of a captain
    Review computer systems

Day Twenty-One: . . . . Approximately 20 minutes
    Reunite any trainees who started together with the captains and managers. Allow
    them to evaluate the training they received and identify any areas where they think
    they need additional training

Trainee	Trainer
Name: _____	Name: _____
	Date: _____

DAY ONE

Trainee should initial each task as completed.

Location: _____

_____ Personnel   _____ Pool/Fitness

_____ Housekeeping   _____ Phone Bank

_____ Service Elevators   _____ Guest Rooms

_____ Gift Shop   _____ Coffee Machine

_____ Conference Services   _____ Front Desk

_____ Banquet Rooms   _____ Valet Desk

_____ Guest Rooms   _____ Banquet Kitchen

_____ Employee Café   _____ Guest Elevators

_____ Employee Locker Room

Introductions:

Introduce yourself to whomever you encounter. Meet as many department heads as possible.

Overview of Manual:

_____ Review Table of Contents

_____ Read Section I—General Information

_____ Read Section II—Your Department

Overview of the Two-Week Training Period:

Receive:

_____ Uniform   _____ Employee Handbook

_____ Name Tag   _____ Crumber

_____ Time Card   _____ Pens

_____ Server Training Manual

_____   _____
Trainer Sign & Date   **Trainee Sign & Date**

Trainee
Name: _____

Trainer
Name: _____

Date: _____

DAY TWO

Trainee should initial each task as completed.

Review Menus:

_____ Breakfast

_____ Lunch

_____ Dinner

_____ Pub

_____ Room Service

Service Style:

_____ Proper Etiquette

_____ Timing

_____ Suggestive Selling

_____ Table Settings

Computers:

_____ Assign ID number

_____ Learn how to begin and pick up tables

_____ Locate various menus, including preps

_____ Practice ordering from various menus

_____ Authorize credit card

_____ Run tip report

_____
Trainer Sign & Date

_____
Trainee Sign & Date

Trainee
Name: _____

Trainer
Name: _____

Date: _____

DAY THREE

Trainee should initial each task as completed.

Cocktail Service:

_____ Learn well, call, and top-shelf brands
(commit to memory)

_____ Learn garnishes of common drinks

_____ Understand bar terms
(e.g., up, rox, flag, muddle, etc.)

_____ Identify common drinks and preps associated with them

_____ Identify ways to upsell

_____ Learn glassware of the bar

_____ Practice ordering various beverages on the computer

Wine Service:

_____ Understand setup of wine list

_____ Identify characteristics of varieties

_____ Read and observe demo of proper wine service

_____ Read and observe demo of champagne service

_____ Locate wines by the glass and by the bottle

_____ Practice presenting, opening, and serving wine until comfortable with correct
procedure

Review Computer System:

Trainer Sign & Date   **Trainee Sign & Date**

Trainee
Name: _____

Trainer
Name: _____

Date: _____

DAY FOUR

Trainee should initial each task as completed.

Follow a captain: _____
Observe every step of service

Learn about French Press Coffee:

_____ What is it?

_____ Learn how to prepare

_____ Available flavors

_____ How to suggestively sell

_____ How to serve

_____ Prepare French Press coffee correctly

Nonalcoholic Beverage Service:

Learn how to present and serve the following:

_____ Hot tea

_____ Hot chocolate

_____ Iced tea & soda

_____ Iced coffee

_____ Juice

_____ Milk

_____	_____
Trainer Sign & Date	**Trainee Sign & Date**

Trainee
Name: _____

Trainer
Name: _____

Date: _____

DAY FIVE

Trainee should initial each task as completed.

Follow a captain: _____

Observe every step of service

Enter All Orders for Your Captain on the Computer

_____ Organize all orders by course

_____ Use correct preps

_____ Separate checks as needed

_____ Authorize credit cards as needed

_____ Recite the well, call, and top-shelf brands

_____ Recite common drinks with their preps and garnishes

_____ Determine ways to suggestively sell

_____   _____

Trainer Sign & Date   **Trainee Sign & Date**

Trainee
Name: _____

Trainer
Name: _____

Date: _____

DAY SIX

Trainee should initial each task as completed.

Follow a captain: _____
Observe every step of service

_____ Review proper table settings
_____ Practice properly setting tables
_____ Learn the art of buffet "fussing"
_____ Provide peels plate and wet naps
_____ Refold napkins
_____ Crumb tables and chairs
_____ Replenish silver
_____ Clear plates

_____   _____
Trainer Sign & Date   **Trainee Sign & Date**

Trainee
Name: _____

Trainer
Name: _____

Date: _____

DAY SEVEN

Trainee should initial each task as completed.

Follow a captain: _____

Observe every step of service

Review Wine List:

_____ Name five (5) wines "2 red, 2 white and 1 blush" that you feel comfortable recommending

_____ Name wines available by the glass

_____ Open wines tableside for your captain's tables or practice opening wine for the bartenders using the house wine

_____ Practice pouring wine into a glass

_____   _____
Trainer Sign & Date   **Trainee Sign & Date**

Trainee   Trainer _____
Name: _____   Name: _____

                                          Date: _____

DAY EIGHT

Trainee should initial each task as completed.

Take 2 or 3 Tables Under the Supervision of a Captain:

_____ Display professional conduct

_____ Warm greeting and farewell

_____ Use open-ended questions

_____ Properly describe buffet and specials

_____ Use proper service etiquette

_____ Suggestively sell whenever possible

_____ Be able to answer guests' questions

_____ Properly reset tables

_____ Proper use of computers

Review:

_____ Nonalcoholic beverages

_____ Wines (house and at least 6 sold by the bottle)

_____   _____
Trainer Sign & Date   **Trainee Sign & Date**

Trainee
Name: _____

Trainer
Name: _____

Date: _____

DAY NINE

Trainee should initial each task as completed.

Take 2 or 3 Tables Under the Supervision of a Captain:

_____ Display professional conduct

_____ Warm greeting and farewell

_____ Use open-ended questions

_____ Properly describe buffet and specials

_____ Use proper service etiquette

_____ Suggestively sell whenever possible

_____ Be able to answer guests' questions

_____ Properly reset tables

_____ Proper use of computers

Review:

Menu:

_____ Identify two appetizers and two entrées you could recommend

_____ Describe sauces

_____ Know accompaniments

_____ Know portion sizes

_____ Know preps to ask

_____ Know the main ingredients

Trainer Sign & Date   **Trainee Sign & Date**

Trainee
Name: _____

Trainer
Name: _____

Date: _____

DAY TEN

Trainee should initial each task as completed.

Take 2 or 3 Tables Under the Supervision of a Captain:

_____ Display professional conduct

_____ Warm greeting and farewell

_____ Use open-ended questions

_____ Properly describe buffet and specials

_____ Use proper service etiquette

_____ Suggestively sell whenever possible

_____ Be able to answer guests' questions

_____ Properly reset tables

_____ Proper use of computers

Review:

_____ Computer system

_____ Location of menus and preps

_____ Separate checks

_____ Authorize credit cards

_____ Run reports

_____
Trainer Sign & Date

_____
Trainee Sign & Date

Trainee
Name: _____

Trainer
Name: _____

Date: _____

DAY TWENTY-ONE

Review

Meet with the trainers and discuss your progress:

_____ Questions

_____ Concerns

_____ Assign mentor

Index